GW00728867

This item must be returned or renewed by the last date shown below. The loan period may be shortened if it is reserved by another reader. A fine will be due if it is not returned on time.

DATE OF RETURN

 3 MAY 1994

THE JEW
IN EARLY ENGLISH
LITERATURE

THE JEW
IN EARLY ENGLISH
LITERATURE

BY

Dr H. MICHELSON

HERMON PRESS
NEW YORK

THE JEW IN EARLY ENGLISH LITERATURE
Reprinted 1972
Hermon Press, New York
L.C.C. No. 72-83940
ISBN 0-87203-035-0

CONTENTS

	Page
Introduction	1
The Old Testament	7
The New Testament	7
Herod	8
His Wroth	8
The Devil	8
Caiaphas	8
Jewish Noisiness	9
Judas	9
The Jews, their Cruelty, Mockery, Cursing, Swearing, etc.	10
The Gospel in Anglo Saxon England	12
The Two Testaments in Anglo-Saxon England	13
Settlement of the Jews in England	16
The Saxons. The Normans. The English Jews	20—21
The Jew from an Economical Point of View. The King and the Jew	23
The Jew's legal Position.	24
The Clergy and the Jew	26
Usury	29
The People and the Jew	31
The Blood-Sacrifice, Murder of Hugh of Lincoln, etc.	32
The Expulsion	35
The Black Death and its Cause	39

Page

The Jew a Mixture of Historical Facts and Biblical Fancy 40

The Jew's Ubiquity in Literature 41

William Langland's Piers Plowman 41

The Miracles of Our Lady in the Vernon Ms. . . 42

Chaucer's Prioressess Tale 43

A Disputation between a Christian and a Jew . . 45

The Pound of Flesh Incident 46

Cursor Mundi 47

John Gower's Confessio Amantis 48

Romances. Titus and Vespasian 49

Anthony Munday's Of a Jew who would for his Debt have a Pound of the Flesh of a Christian 49

The Ballads: Judas. St. Stephan and Herod. The Harrowing of Hell. The Jew's Daughter. The Wandering Jew. . . . . 49—53

The Religious Drama; Mystery and Miracle. . . 54—55

Gesticulation, Jargon, Wroth, Bragging and Cruelty 58—59

The Jew's Comic Character 60

Play of Sacrament 61

The Morality 62

St. Mary Magdalen 63

Devil, Vice and Jew 65

The Regular Drama. Wilson's Three Ladies of London 66

„The Jew" 69

Marlowe's Jew of Malta 70

Machiavelli 70

Shylock 82

Massinger's Duke of Milan and Machiavellus . . 85—86

Greene's Selimus 86

The Wisdom of Doctor Dodypoll 87

Jacke Drum's Entertainement 87

Page

The Travailes of the Three English Brothers . . .   88
Robert Daborne's A Christian turned Turk. . .   90
Decker's Jew of Venice and Newes from Hell. .91—92
Beaumont and Fletcher's Custom of the Country .   92
Webster's The Devil's Law-Case   94
Thomas Goffe's The Raging Turk   94
John Ford's Perkin Warbeck   95
Richard Brome's The Jewish Gentleman   95
Peele's The Love of King David and Fair Bethsabe   96
William Hemings. The Jewes Tragedy   96
The name of „Jew"   96
The Jew's Bearing and Physiognomy   97
   „   „   Body   102
   „   „   Dress   103
   „   „   Smell   106
   „   „   Language, Swearing and Cursing . .   106
   „   „   Soul and Character.   107
   „   „   Aim in Life and Mode of Living . .   111
   „   „   Criminality   113
   „   „   Intellect and Learning   115
   „   „   House   120
   „   „   Family   122
   „   „   Servants   128
   „   „   Friends   129
   „   „   Philanthropy   130
   „   „   Religion   131
   „   „   Money   134
   „   „   Occupation   136
Racial Hatred, Competition and Intolerance . . .   141
The Jew's Life among the Christians   144
The Law and the Jew   146
Jew-Baiting   149

  Page

Baptism 150

*Probability of the Jew's Character in Literature
  from a Jewish Point of View* 153

*Probability of the Jew's Character in Literature
  from a general point of view* 157

Reason of the Jew's Success on the Stage 163

*The Jew's Change from a Comic figure to a Tragi-
  Comic one* 164

Devil and Vice 166

*An Appreciation of the Jew in the Drama from a
  purely technical point of view* 167

Conclusion 171

*Principal Books, Pamphlets, Periodicals, Texts,
  Essays, Literary Histories, Books of Reference,
  referred to.* 174

"Aaron fil diaboli" Aaron, Son of the Devil. Photograph of a part of an
entry on the Forest Roll of Essex, 5 Ed. I. (1277) now at the Record Office.
The portrait or caricature is the earliest dated sketch of a mediæval Jew.
The badge on the dress represents the Two Tables of the Law, which all
Jews were obliged to wear in saffron taffity.

THE JEW
IN EARLY ENGLISH
LITERATURE

INTRODUCTION

This very day, Friday 17 October 1924, I have read an article in the "Handelsblad" on the "Z. R. III" on the accomplishment of her glorious passage across the Ocean and my heart leapt up at this wonderful achievement. How deeply mortified I felt, when I came upon the following passage: "One paper wrote (of course a national-socialistic one, under the auspices of the great general Ludendorff): The rumour is now spreading in the democratic and social-democratic press that Dr.... of the Zeppelin-works at Friedrichshaven is the builder of the "Z. R. III" and that with his staff of engineers he will shortly go to the New World by boat. This is a lie. Dr..... is only a subordinate official. He is 50 % Jew and that is also the reason why he was not on board the airship. If he had not been a Jew and had really built the Zeppelin, he would have had courage enough to fly with her instead of taking the safe steamer." My subject is the Jew in Early English Literature and the above quotation illustrates the Jew in Modern German Journalism and though a period of about five centuries separates the two Jews, we see that they are still strongly connected by the chain of hatred that was forged for them some nineteen centuries ago.

This dissertation is the natural outcome of a circumstance that has set its mark upon my whole life. When-

Michelson

ever I came into contact with Christians directly or indirectly, personally or in literature, I was generally [1] struck by the animosity, disdain, distrust, aloofness or at any rate a hardly definable yet clearly perceptible reserve on their side and I have always thought of and looked for any ground that justified this attitude, but in vain. As a student of English literature it was the very same thing and I resolved to sift the matter there, which I have done in this dissertation and I am glad to say with the same result, so that without any such intention on my side it has also become an attempt at the vindication and justification of the Jew in Early English Literature.

In the very earliest stages of their cultural development the differences between the progenitors of the various races must have been minute. The minute differences influenced by the differences of time, place and opportunity, developed and ultimately resulted in different systems of culture and these systems hold mankind in their iron grips and prevent a universal amalgamation.

When using the word 'man' we think of creatures distinguished from all other creatures by certain characteristics which they have in common. Closer investigation, however, at once reveals that we have included in the word 'man', an immense number of beings, two of which are not alike. Between these two extremes of looking upon mankind as one individual and upon every individual as a world in himself, lie hundreds of

---

[1] I want to emphasize this 'generally' for I have often come across persons who were entirely free from anti-semitism, either on account of their true Christian spirit, or because they were far above those distinctions between man and man that act as diseases which split up what should be one great brotherhood.

classifications, grouping more or less heterogeneous or homogeneous masses into races, nations, tribes, classes, sects, parties, sets, etc. From the very outset every honest investigator knows that the limits between these groups are vague and hazy, that there are no clear lines of demarcation and that general assertions based upon these classifications must be accepted with the greatest reserve. It is practically nonsense to say the Dutch are a clean nation, or the French a patriotic one, that the Italians are treacherous or the Germans faithful, the Red Indians heroes, and the Jews cowards, for this would imply that no Dutchman could be patriotic, no Frenchman clean, no Italian faithful, no German treacherous, no Red Indian a coward, no Jew a hero. We must therefore proceed with the greatest reserve in tracing what we call racial, national or tribal peculiarities.

Of course a negro on the outside is quite different from an Englishman. Inside, clever anatomists may be able to trace minute differences and we may safely assume that there are minuter differences in their spiritual composition which would not escape the psychologist. Nevertheless, although a negro-baby adopted and practically from its birth educated by Englishmen in England, will never become an Englishman to outward appearances, and although some innate spiritual qualities will stick to him for life, he will become an Englishman from a cultural point of view. Provision must be made of course for the fact, that his being black and differently featured will so often be brought home to him that he will believe himself to be a negro after all, in spite of his English culture. If by some process we could make him look like an ordinary Englishman, however, he would think himself one and pass for one in spite of some spiritual peculiarities that would be looked upon as personal traits.

Let us now pass on to the Jews. Notwithstanding their semitic origin a vast number of them might easily pass for Christian inhabitants of Southern Europe and not a few even for natives of any part of Europe. So their outward appearance forms no obstacle for assimilation. In their case it is only their ancient culture and its consequences that has made them and still makes them stand apart and that will continue to do so, unless the great miracle shall happen one day, the dream of so many idealists, the miracle by which all cultures will be thrown aside as so many worthless worn out garments and man will stand naked and innocent as Adam stood in Paradise, with this difference that the new Adam will know that he is naked and glory in it. A new and all-embracing culture.

The purpose of this essay is not to prove the final superiority of the Jews over Christians, nor even their ultimate similarity in the essentials of Life. Any systematic comparison between Jews and Christians will be avoided. Problems of religion and race will be only incidentally touched and then only as far as they are reflected in Literature and History together. The purpose is simply to trace the Jew, as he figures in early English literature and to compare the results of this research with what History has to say on these points; so a comparison of literary facts and historical facts concerning the Jew, avoiding general assertions as much as possible. I further intend to show that the New

Testament and nothing but the New Testament is to be blamed for the peculiar psychology of the Jew in literature, that down to and inclusive of Shylock this psychology was never based on observation, but simply taken over from the New Testament and handed down for centuries through all sorts of phases of literature. To this imaginary psyche was added something that resembled a Jew in his outward appearance and was based upon superficial contemporary observation of the Jew in the Diaspora. We must of course expect that some real Jewish traits have likewise been observed and added to the literary creation.

I am afraid that in the course of my essay I shall ruffle the mind of some people, when I shall be writing about the Gospel as if it were an ordinary book, written by ordinary mortals. With Luther I must say, I cannot act otherwise, and as compensation I am glady prepared to acknowledge the beauty of the true Christian Spirit and Idealism which are likewise to be found there. I am afraid that in the course of my study I shall also ruffle the mind of some other people, when I shall admit certain unpleasant Jewish peculiarities, for which I atone at once by confessing my heartfelt sympathy with their numerous and far-reaching good ones.

When disproving the representation of the Jewish psyche found in the New Testament, I am in a way backed by an eminent religious Christian historian the Rev. Henry Hart Milman, Dean of St. Paul's, who says of the Jews:

"The functions which they have performed in the progress of human development and civilization are so important, so enduring; their barbarism has been so fiercely and contemptuously exaggerated, their premature wisdom and humanity so contemptuously depreciated or denied that is as impossible, as it would be unwise to limit full freedom of inquiry."

It may be asked why I speak of the Jew in general and why I call this essay the "Jew" in Early Literature. This is because there is a striking similarity in the Jews occurring there, being all built up of three elements: a soul created by prejudice, outward appearances, and traits of secondary importance. This makes even such a seemingly complicate character as Shylock into a Type.

It will be my constant care not to lose sight of the fact that, although the Jew may be represented in a thoroughly caricatured, perverted, false and unhistorical way, he need not at all be badly drawn from an artistic point of view, just as little as a Jew represented in a true historical manner, must needs be artistically portrayed. We may have a highly artistic perversion of what is looked upon as truth and superlatively insipid reality.

THE JEW IN EARLY ENGLISH LITERATURE

The Old Testament. — If we want to understand literary creations like Gernutus and the Jew's Daughter, Barabas and Abigail or Shylock and Jessica, if we want to understand the Jew in early English literature, then it is absolutely necessary to go back to the Book of Books, the Holy Bible containing the Old and New Testaments, and see what we find there about the son of Jehuda. There, in his cradling-place ,we shall surely find the first traces that will enable us to follow him on his wanderings through the realms of letters, which are a faithful though faint reflection of his sorrowful wanderings through the real world. Genesis! The gigantic figures rise before us as depicted in the impressive holy tongue. Exodus! Others of equal power follow. Adam, Eve, Abel, Noah, Abraham, Isaac, Jacob, Joseph, Moses, David, Esther, Job, Judith and a great many more. Sublime figures that strike us dumb with reverence and awe or make us burst out in eloquent admiration by their innate grandeur. Christian and Jew alike undergo their influence.

The New Testament. — The mighty names that followed Genesis and Exodus have ended with Malachi and a new sound is heard. The voice of Matthew cries "Jesus Christ, the son of David, the son of Abraham" and the awful name strikes doubt in the hearts of some and certainty in the hearts of many, certainty of eternal bliss on one side and certainty of an unholy deception on the other side. And those in whose hearts certainty of eternal bliss descended called themselves Christians after Jesus Christ and those in whose heart certainty of an unholy deception dwelt, retained their old name of Jews, which became a stigma in the eyes of the others.

Herod. — Now when Jesus was born Herod was troubled and all Jerusalem with him and he sent the wise men to Bethlehem and said, go and search out exactly concerning the young child that I may also come and worship him. Here is the first Jew seen in the new light, the subtle, treacherous liar never fair and square, the dealer of underhanded blows. How maliciously he adds "and when ye have found him, bring me word, that I may also come and worship him".

Worship him, indeed, where he only sought the young child to destroy it!

His wroth. — Then Herod, when he saw that he was mocked of the wise men, was exceeding wroth and no doubt he raged as all Jews are said to rage and are shown to rage in literature. And then the Jew Herod's cruelty in slaying all the male children that were in Bethlehem from two years and under!

The Devil. — Before dealing with the other Jewish enemies of the Lord, enemies born of women, we must first mention one of nobler extraction, the fallen archangel, proud Lucifer, who tempted him sorely in the wilderness and is thus placed on a par with the Jews.

Caiaphas. — When Jesus' influence had grown, then were gathered together the chief priests, and the elders of the people, unto the court of the high priest, who was called Caiaphas; and they took counsel together that they might take Jesus by subtlety, and kill him. Now here are Jews of the true stamp. The same subtlety [1] that characterizes Herod is found again in them at their attempt to take the life of Jesus: what cannot be obtained by fair shall be obtained by foul means and they seek false witnesses against Jesus.

Jewish Noisiness. — Those Jews were always a noisy and loud people. Was not Herod loud in his wroth and is not the high priest loud in his pretended indignation? How he rends his garments and how the council spit in the face of Jesus and buffet him, while some smite him with the palms of their hands when he is tried before the Sanhedrin.

Judas. — A very Jew is Judas the hypocrite, the thief, the swindler (John, 12), the traitor. Judas Iscariot, who went up to the chief priests and said: what are ye willing to give me, and I will deliver Him unto you? And they weighed unto him thirty pieces of silver. With a simple question the utter baseness of this Jew's soul is laid bare. When sitting at meat with the twelve disciples, Jesus said: "verily I say unto you that one of you shall betray me". And they were exceeding sorrowful, and began to say unto him every one, Is it I, Lord and also Judas said: "Is it I, Rabbi?" Quite in keeping with his character is the way in which he betrays Him. With a kiss! Now he that betrayed Him gave them a sign, saying, whomsoever I shall kiss that is He: take Him. And straightway he came to Jesus, and said: 'Hail, Rabbi' and kissed him. That this Judas repented and

[1] See: Jewish Criminality.

hanged himself shows that his new faith had left some impression upon him.

The Jews, their Cruelty, Mockery, Cursing, Swearing, etc. — The Jews are cruel to a degree, for when Jesus was crucified, they that passed by railed on him, wagging their heads and mocking him, so did the chief priests, the scribes and the elders and when in his agony Jesus cried with a loud voice: "Eli, Eli, lama sabachthani?" some cruel Jews mocked him and straightway one of them ran, and took a sponge, and filled it with vinegar, and put it on a reed, and gave him to drink. When the Roman soldiers came with the miraculous news of Jesus' resurrection, the chief priests and the elders gave them much money, saying, say ye, his disciples came by night, and stole him away while we slept. Another interesting feature of the Jews is revealed when Peter, who is recognized by his speech, which no doubt is understood to have been meek and gentle, as of one of the followers of Christ, wants to deny that he is such a one and begins to curse and swear, which no doubt demonstrates the fact that the real Jew was a creature accustomed to cursing and swearing. This then is the character of the Jew as depicted in the Gospel. A creature full of subtlety and treachery, a dealer of underhanded blows, a liar, a cruel, malicious fellow, a mocker, a murderer, a hypocrite, a traitor, a coward, covetous, boisterous, loud and haughty. I deem it quite superfluous to demonstrate the absurdity of this characterization of the Jews, for the slightest acquaintance with their history at once refutes this portrayal. If we are to judge the Jews of that time, we cannot but admit that their ancient culture and degree of civilization could stand comparison with those of the contemporary nations, and that they of all peoples should consist of a small number of righteous persons and an overwhelming majority of devilish scoundrels, is a view so ludicrous that I may abstain from further comment. But how are we to account for this contorted and false representation. Was this done on purpose? I think not. Zeal is often called blind and history has taught us over and over again until this very day that the zealous apostles of new creeds have never been able to see any good in the adherents to the other creeds which they wanted to overthrow or modify. The Gospel is the propaganda of a new religion or at least a modification of an old one, so we need not be surprised at the little esteem in which the adherents to the latter are held by its propagandists The above-mentioned catalogue of sins is the stock in trade of any people and any faith except those of the Christians and when, in his Epistle to the Romans, Paul enumerates the sins that make Gentiles and Jews alike stand in need of righteousness, we find them tally pretty closely with those already discussed, for Gentiles and Jews are "filled with all unrighteousness, wickedness, covetousness, maliciousness, envy, murder, strife, deceit, malignity; whisperers, backbiters; hateful to God; insolent, haughty, boastful; inventors of evil things, covenant-breakers; without natural affection, unmerciful." [1] Before taking leave of the New Testament, it will serve our purpose to point out that, if the enemies of the Lord and his followers are possessed of the blackest vices, the Son of God and his faithful followers are the personifications of the

[1] *Epistle of Paul to the Romans*, 1. 29—31.

most unspotted virtues: righteousness, goodness, unselfishness, liberality, benevolence, peaceableness, straightforwardness, purity, humility, wisdom, etc.

The Gospel in Anglo-Saxon England. — As I have already said, it is absolutely necessary to take due note of the Jew as we find him in the Old and New Testaments and especially in the latter. For this was the Gospel and it was Gospel truth that the zealous preachers took to England. Those priests were no critical scholars or scientists of the twentieth century. They were rather soldiers in a holy war who had received orders from their holy king to go and conquer the whole world. "It was not theirs to reason why, it was theirs to do and die." To them every word of the New Testament was Gospel truth and it would have been lost labour for any scientist, if there had been one, to try and show the Jew from another point of view. Such was the priest, the preacher, the teacher, such was his teaching, and even as they were they towered high above the Anglo-Saxon heathens and their heathendom. The mind of the Anglo-Saxon was virgin soil in which the priests planted the seeds of the Gospel and the exotic garden of the East soon filled this Western Isle. It was in 597 that Christianity was brought into England by Augustine. In doing so he could not but bring the Jew along with it, that is to say not the Jew of flesh and blood, but the Jew of the New Testament, the enemy of the founder of the Christian creed.

Is is true, my subject is not Religion but Literature. At the outset, however, these two practically coincide. English Literature in its infancy was suckled with Christian religion, the influence of which it has hardly

ever shaken off in its later periods. As a matter of fact
Religion was practically warp and woof in Anglo-Saxon
literature. I can do no better than quote Saintsbury [1]
on this point, who says that "as regards Anglo-Saxon
literature especially its poetry we may say that it is
Christian in tone and definitely religious in subject.
Probably not a twentieth part of the Corpus Poeticum
in oldest English has for subject anything but paraphrases of the Bible and Lives of Saints, which in their turn
are paraphrased or translated from Latin originals and
it would have been extremely surprising, if anything
else had been the case. It is the literature of a childhood, the lisping of a people. What culture there was,
centred chiefly in the clergy and the monasteries. In the
first years (which in such an age are the first centuries)
of conversion to a new faith religious zeal thinks no
subject but religion worthy of attention."

The Two Testaments in Anglo-Saxon England. —
Beside the translations of the two Testaments we see a
prose- and poetry-literature grow up in the Anglo-Saxon
tongue. The story of the creation of the world is retold
in prose and verse. Of course a change has taken place
especially in verse, where together with the language
something of the Anglo-Saxon spirit has invaded the
venerable story. This is illustrated by the Cædmonic
Exodus, which breathes a very warlike spirit, though it
must have been written by a monk and though no
actual battle is described. Moses is quite an Anglo-
Saxon leader. Similar in spirit is a poem based upon the
Apocryphal book of Judith, of which poem we have
only the end, describing the slaughter of Holofernes and

[1] Saintsbury, *Short History of English Literature* pp. 9/10.

the triumph of the warlike Jews. On the whole we must say that the Jews of the Old Testament are looked upon with the same reverence by Christians and Jews alike. Anglo-Saxon literature closely follows the Old Testament and only infuses its own spirit into it. The Anglo-Saxons even went a step too far in their reverence and in *Solomon and Saturn* they made Solomon stand for Christian wisdom and tell Saturn of the power of the paternoster.

The Jew of the Old Testament is dealt with in a way entirely different from the one in which his lineal descendant the Jew of the New Testament is treated, or his later offspring the Jew of the diaspora, both uncouth aliens in the realm of literature down to modern times. The Jews before Christ's birth *could* not be considered bad Jews. They could not be redeemed from the original sin, as no Saviour had as yet arisen for this purpose. Original sin lies on them like a heavy burden, it is true, but the Son of Man will come, willing to take their sins upon Him; they were doomed, but their redemption was near at hand. They were no enemies of the Lord, who suffered for their sake. He was not cruelly tortured by them. They were not bad, far from it, they were even classified among the Saints, for in Ælfric's *Lives of Saints*, the Kings and heroes of the Old Testament come in for a share. We may say that the biblical stories about Adam and Eve, Abel, Noah, Abraham and Sarah, Isaac, Jacob, Joseph, Moses, Joshua, the Judges, Ruth, Samuel, Esther, Job, Judith, Elias, Daniel, etc., etc., were introduced into Anglo-Saxon literature, passed through Middle English and early Modern English and as a matter of fact have been handed down to modern times never losing their close contact with their sources.

But everything changes for the Jew as soon as we come to the contemporaries of Jesus. Then we have again to distinguish between those who are on the side of the Saviour and those who are against Him. Little need be said about those who are on His side, for they are no longer Jews, they have become Christians, but woe unto those who are against Him, they are looked upon and treated in quite a different manner.

In heathen times Literature generally had the same subject. In pagan poetry the story turns round a hero, whose struggles with all sorts of enemies are chanted. The best Anglo-Saxon example of a song in praise of a hero is no doubt the Beowulf. In 681 all the Anglo-Saxon tribes had become Christians and the heroes of pagan times had to give way to the hero of heroes and the ancient enemies vanished to make room for the enemy of enemies, the arch-fiend and his rout. In the very earliest Christian poetry Jesus figures as a hero, he is a mighty warrior fighting the Devil. He outshines the old heathen hero, the conqueror of the old dragons, for He conquers the root of all evil, he conquers Satan. The militant side of the Christian religion attracted the Anglo-Saxons. The battlefield is shifted from fens and moors and other dangerous places to Hell, but the old idea of good battling against evil has remained. Nor do the combating immortals lack their followers. In the opening lines of the *Andreas*, Christ and his twelve disciples are described as a warrior prince and his doughty followers. Jesus, the Son of God, is surrounded by Angels in heaven and Lucifer, the son of Darkness, is swarmed about by the spirits of Evil in hell, and on earth we find the Apostles and Christians following the cross and the non-Christians especially the Jews with their priests and King are equally faithful adherents of the Devil. The fiendish character of the Jew is therefore found not only in the translations and paraphrases of the New Testament, but also in the literary productions based on them, as well as in the homilies by Ælfric and Wulfstan. "Ealle gesceafta oncneowon heora Scyppendes tocyme, buton þam arleasum Iudeiscum anum." The heavens, the sea, the sun, the earth and even hell know it. "And þeah þa heardheortan Iudei noldon for eallum þam tacnum þone soþan Scyppend tocnawan." [1]

Settlement of the Jews in England. — This was the Jew of Anglo-Saxon literature. This was the attitude of those who made this literature before the Jews settled in England and from all this we may safely conclude that the sentiments of the Anglo-Saxons towards the Jews were far from friendly before they actually knew them and the fact that the race of the murderers of the Lord should come in the train of the foreign Conqueror, was not exactly fit to mollify the feelings of the conquered and oppressed barbarians. Small wonder then that the fair-haired, ignorant Anglo-Saxons looked with a mingling of terror [2] and hate upon the swarthy, cunning Hebrew with whom they had hardly anything in common, as he dressed differently and spoke either the language of the Conqueror or even worse, some stranger tongue more in keeping with his being. Nor did the relation improve on better acquaintance. The son of

[1] H. Sweet, *Selected Homilies of Ælfric*, pp. 27/28.
[2] The Jews were also feared in some degree. This is expressed by Fernese in *The Jew of Malta:* "I always feared that Jew". *Everyman's Library*, p. 213.

Jehuda, the man of travel, learning and property, looked down upon them as uncultured barbarians, vile creatures without any education, a people whose nobility is described as much addicted to lust and gluttony, and all its ranks as given to excessive drinking, the common vice of all, in which they spent nights and days without intercession. Men with whom the Jew did not join at meals, whose daughters were objects of abomination to him. Rather would he see his own daughter dead before him than give her in marriage even to the best man among them. It mattered little that this Jew gave an impulse to industry such as England had never felt before, for England could not appreciate it. What did matter was the heavy usury he necessarily exacted in the general insecurity of the time and forced by the heavy taxes he had to pay to the King. It mattered little that chiefly through him trade flourished to such a degree that the barter system of England gave way to the modern trade for money and towns flourished and grew in population and prosperity; what mattered was that little by little he became the unofficial taxgatherer in a system of indirect taxation, in which he was an instrument in the King's hand, a sucking spongelike instrument, which first drained the country owing to the monopoly of capitalist transactions given to him by the Canon Law and then could be squeezed into the Royal Treasury. It mattered little that through him a change was brought about in architecture and that buildings of stone were built instead of squalid wooden houses, and that there was scarcely an important building in the country which was not raised by means of Jewish capital and that the buildings, which, as at Lincoln and St. Edmundsbury, still retain their title of "Jews' Houses", were almost the first houses of stone, which superseded the mere hovels of the English burghers. What did matter was that in these houses Jews could alas blaspheme and crucify Christian children to their hearts' content and store the wealth which they were supposed to derive from draining the people. Little were they esteemed because they opened a way for the revival of physical science and perhaps even founded a medical school at Oxford. In spite of this and in spite of all they remained the Jews of the New Testament and the literature based on it.

The Jew, who was a scholar, an industrial and commercial genius at the same time, [1] made the air, earth and oceans flower into wisdom, comfort and affluence. So it may easily be understood that they were looked upon as magicians. If the romance of science, industry and commerce is more than a fata morgana, if it is really the true story of the development of mankind, then some honour is due to the Jew, who was never to be found in the rear of those who helped to supply the subject matter of this romance. But if even in our enlightened time we feel some hidden power behind great scholars, industrial and commercial geniuses, how then is it to be wondered at, that ignorant barbarians should actually see real sorcery and witchcraft behind the Jew. Poor magician! "There is a fatality about all distinction and it is better not to be too different from one's fellow creatures" (Oscar Wilde).

As regards the Jew's settlement I have been able to trace the following data and dates.

[1] Encyclopaedia Britannica p. 40, on the Jews.

In *A History of the Jews in England* Albert M. Hyamson [1] mentions the possibility that Jews came already with the Phoenicians and remained in Britain. Salomon Goldschmidt in *Geschichte der Juden in England im XI. und XII. Jahrhundert* [2] thinks it probable that they came with Rome's legions, established commercial relations and even founded a Jewish colony in London. These, however, are mere suppositions, though not at all out of keeping with the enterprising spirit of the Jews, which manifested itself so splendidly before, during, and after the Middle Ages and which has characterized them until the present day.

The first certainty about Jews in England we find at the end of the 7th century in the *Liber poenitentialis*, in the ancient laws and institutes of England, [3] by Archbishop Theodorus of Canterbury, who speaks about measures to regulate the intercourse between Jews and Christians, with which also compare Venerabilis Bedae *Historia Ecclesiastica Gentis Anglorum*. Certain proof we also derive from the 146th paragraph of the Canonical Excerptions published by Ecgbriht, Archbishop of York, in the year 740, which forbids any Christians to be present at the Jewish feasts [4]. The learned Spelman is of opinion that their settlement in England is traceable in the notice taken of them in the laws of Edward the Confessor (1004—1066) which, amongst other things, declare that Judæi, et omnia sua regis sunt [4]. There are those who say, however, that the above-mentioned

[1] Publ. by Chatto and Windus, London, 1908, pp. 1—2.
[2] Leipzig Diss. 1886, p. 1.
[3] Ed. by Benjamin Thorpe, London 1840, Vol. II pp. 1—62.
[4] D'Blossiers, *Anglia Judaica*. Milman, *Hist. of the Jews*, Vol. III, p. 229, where futher proofs are given.

laws, institutes, excerptions, may have been bodily taken over from continental ones and thus lose their value
as proofs of any Jewish settlement before 1068, when the
Jews followed William the Conqueror from Normandy to
remain in England freely till 1290 [1] and then covertly
till the reign of Cromwell [2] and then openly again until
the present day. It cannot be but useful to note the
state the country was in at about the time of the
settlement of the Jews, for it will throw some light upon
their position among its inhabitants.

When first the latter became known to the Tyrian
mariners, they were, if we are to believe Macaulay,
little superior to the natives of the Sandwich Islands.
They were next subjugated by the Roman arms; but they
received only a faint tincture of Roman arts and letters.

The Saxons. — Then the Saxons conquered Britain
and the conquered race became as barbarous as the
conquerors. A new step in the development of the inhabitants of England was their conversion to Christianity, but a very strange sort of Christianity it was,
deeply corrupted as it was by everything against which
it had long contended. This Christianity tried to oust the
brute violence, audacity of spirit and fierceness that had
hitherto reigned and just when civilization began to rise,
it was almost completely wiped out again by the invasion
of the Danish heathen.

"Still, at the date of the Conquest the country was
undoubtedly in regard to everything intellectual in a
very backward state. Ordericus Vitalis, almost a contemporary writer, and himself a native of England,

[1] Green, *A Short History the English People.*
[2] Sources to be mentioned later on.

though educated abroad, describes his countrymen generally as having been found by the Normans a rustic and almost illiterate people. The last epithet may be understood as chiefly intended to characterize the clergy, for the great body of the laity at this time were illiterate everywhere." [1]

The Normans. And now as regards the Norman [2]. Originally not a trifle better than the Anglo-Saxon or Dane he invaded the Frank empire, where he conquered by his dauntless valour. Once settled he underwent the civilizing influence of the people he had vanquished. Instead of his squalid native hut he learned to build castles, his brutal intemperance, coarse voracity and drunkenness he gave up for polite luxury, banquets delicate rather than abundant. He acquired knowledge and refinement, which resulted in legislation, poetry and romance. He was distinguished by his graceful bearing and insinuating address, skill in negotiation and eloquence, but he had retained his ferocious military spirit.

The Jews in England. — I have shown the chief characteristics of the Anglo-Saxon and Norman. Now let me try to show the Jew as he must probably have figured at that time. It is no good to represent him as he figures in the New Testament for obvious reasons already mentioned, nor as he figures in the Old Testament, for he had been in exile for ages and his character had no doubt adapted itself to the prevailing circumstances. From an independent nation the Jews had become a wandering multitude, settling where settlement was possible and driven forth again when their powerful

[1] G. L. Craik, *A Manual of English Literature and Language*, p. 51.
[2] Macaulay, *Hist. of England*; Green, *A Short Hist. of the English People* and *Encyclopaedia Britannica* (in which Geoffrey Malaterra, 1. 3., is quoted).

hosts could no longer get on with their weak guests. The Jews who had lived in a highly civilized state, now lived dispersed among nations with whom brutal force was a chief virtue. In an essay on Machiavelli, Macaulay gives an explanation of the difference between the nature of the rude nations which lay beyond the Alps and the cultured Italians, which explanation is generalized by him and which, with some modifications, we may apply to the Jews and the nations with which they sojourned. I shall closely follow Macaulay's arguments.

Among the rude Anglo-Saxons, the less rude Normans and the other fierce nations of Europe valour was absolutely indispensable. Without it none could be eminent, few could be secure. Cowardice was therefore naturally considered as the foulest reproach. Among the polished Jews, enriched by commerce, governed by Mosaical and Rabbinical Law and passionately attached to its study and study in general, everything was done by superiority of intelligence. Their success in life required civil rather than military qualifications. Hence, while courage was the point of honour among the nations mentioned above, ingenuity became the point of honour among the Jews. From these principles were deduced, by processes strictly analogous, two opposite systems of fashionable morality. Among the Anglo-Saxons, for example, the characteristics which peculiarly belong to timid dispositions, and which are the natural defence of weakness, were most disreputable. The Jews held them in high esteem. Such characteristics were self-command, address, quick observation, fertile invention and profound knowledge of human nature. I must at once admit that excesses of these qualities will frequently have occurred among the Jews and will perhaps have been treated by some of them with indulgence. Self-command may easily degenerate into hypocrisy, address into manipulation, fertile invention into fraud and quick observation and profound knowledge of human nature may easily be applied to one's own advantage only. As it was the sad fate of the Jews that among them the innocent had always to suffer with the guilty, this was no doubt the reason why the whole race was represented in literature as habitual cowards, hypocrites and deceivers. This was the outside. As the intercourse between Jews and Christians was restricted to the outside, the latter never became aware of the domestic virtues in which the Jews excelled and only grudgingly admitted their tribal unity and readiness to help each other.

So this is our Jew, the representative of the Semitic race, the bearer of culture and civilisation, the worshipper of one God, the confessor of monotheism in its strictest form, the man of travel, varied learning and property. The intemperance of the Saxon is an abomination to him, even more so than to the Norman, for his Mosaic law forbids it; on the other hand he lacks and is averse to the ferocious spirit of both Norman and Saxon, for he is a man of peace, a trader, a merchant, who does not come with violence and arms to rob and ruin. He comes to sell and buy. His capital is at the disposal of him who wants it and who is able to pay the market price.

The Jew from an economical point of view. The Jews and the King. — In Green's Short History of the English People [1] we find an account of the settlement of the Jews in England, based partly on the *Anglia Judaica*

[1] Green, *A short Hist.* etc., Chapter II, Sec. V.

of Toovey, which gives some account of the Jewish colonies. The following extracts will give a glimpse of the esteem in which they were held when they were there and of their social position.

"William (the Conqueror) found a more ready source of revenue in the settlement of the Jewish traders, who followed him from Normandy, and who were enabled by the royal protection to establish themselves in separate quarters or "Jewries" of the chief towns of England."

So we see that the Jew had to pay heavily for the right of living in England and that he came in the first place as a trader, a merchant. Besides the payment the king received, there was another advantage for him. The Jew was going to assist him in changing the backward state of the country into a modern condition, for England was still in a purely agrarian state and it was William's plan that it should become a country where trade, commerce and industry flourished. Pioneers with capital were necessary for this and as the Jew was the capitalist of that time, he was the right man in the right place.

His legal position. — Now one might expect such a valuable person to be in an extraordinarily favourable legal position. On the contrary! The Norman was a clever negotiator. The Jew could make profits, but if any privileges in that respect were granted him, the advantages should be the Norman's. So these profits were the bait and if the Jew wanted to obtain them, the Norman stipulated that the "profiteer" should place himself in the King's power. The Jew had no right or citizenship in the land [1]. He was simply the King's chattel, and his life and goods

[1] Marlowe, *Jew of Malta*, Act I. Barabas: Are strangers with your tribute to be taxed.

were absolutely at the King's mercy. And this mercy was far from tender. The wealth which he accumulated through his industry was wrung from him, whenever the Crown [1] had need of it, and torture [2] and imprisonment were resorted to, if milder entreaties failed. It was the gold of the Jew that filled the royal exchequer at the outbreak of war or of revolt. Thus the Jew was in the following awkward predicament. On one side the King stood, the Christian King stripping him in a cruel way of his profits, on the other side the people who saw the Jew becoming rich, as they thought, at their expense; both king and people were unanimous in their hatred of the Jew, the former in spite of, the latter on account of his profits.

King John fined a Jew 10000 marks of silver and commanded that he should lose one of his teeth daily till he paid it and in this way the Jew lost seven teeth. The generality of them, we find in contemporary history [3] had one eye put out, hence the expression 'worth a Jewess' eye' (Merchant of Venice II, 5, 42). King Henry III [4] and his Queen fleeced Aaron, a Jew of York, of above 30000 Marks in the space of seven years and shortly before his death [4] the King called upon the Jews "to make up the whole accompt, and pay in the Ballance. All arrears of Talliage were to be cleared in four Months and half of them paid in seventeen days, and in the mean time such as could not give security were to be imprisoned and no otherwise bailed than by body for body and if any of them or their sureties, did

[1] Marlowe, *Jew of Malta*, Act I. The tribute money of the Turks shall all be levied amongst the Jews, and each of them to pay one half of his estate.
[2] Cf. the origin of the expression 'worth a Jewess' eye'·(*Merch. of Venice II*, 5, 42).
[3] Matthew Paris.
[4] Toovey, page 196.

not clear the whole, upon the day prefixed, any sums
formerly paid in part, were to be forfeited, and their
persons, goods and chatels were to be at the King's
mercy. Numbers of them, upon this occasion, were imprisoned in the Tower of London and other places.
Nothing but weeping and wailing, was to be seen in
every corner. Even the friars who had so lately taken
possession of their Synagogue pitied them, nor were the
Caursini [1] and Caturcensian brokers (though their rivals in extortion) without compassion, for nothing could
be more rigorous and unmerciful than the King's pro-
ceedings at this time." King Edward went a step further
and taxed Jewish children as well as their parents.

The Jew and the Clergy. — Nor was the relation between the Clergy and the Jews any better. When Ordericus Vitalis called the clergy illiterate, he meant the
Anglo-Saxon clergy, no doubt. The average Norman
priest, however, was little more erudite. He had a heavy
task. His Anglo-Norman flock was Christian, but very
thin their Christian varnish lay and very transparent it
was, showing but too clearly the heathen colours underlying. The coming of the Jew was sadly ill-timed, he
was sure to thwart his work, for in learning the Jew
was a match for him. What could the priests do but
expose him in the way in which the New Testament did?
They keep Jesus' wounds fresh, keep them bleeding
and at the same time do not allow the people to forget
who caused that precious blood to flow. No doubt the
Jews gave them much trouble in their religious work

[1] Toovey. The Pope was wont to carry on that infamous trade, usury by the help
of several Italian Merchants called Caursini, the Pope's bankers, p. 123. The
Caturcensians were similar people engaged in similar affairs, but came from
southern France, p. 159.

and much anxiety and perhaps a little fear. What with one thing and what with another they hated the Jew fanatically and, as literature was chiefly in their hands, this hatred crops up everywhere in the homilies, the chronicle, the ballad and other poetry, the mystery and miracle. They continued to repeat what they knew from the Gospel, added all disadvantageous matters they gathered from their contemporary social conditions and infused it into the people.

If the Jews had given up their creed, their anomalous position among the Christians would have come to an end for it was their creed, not their race which determined their situation down to the Middle Ages.[1] Thus, for instance, in Angevin England every part of the national life was, at least formally, Christianized, so was the manner of obtaining a farm, so were the guilds, so was trade, so were public or municipal offices. [2]

The reader must not infer from this that the kingdom of Christ was established here, far from it. As I have already said Christianity was but a veneer covering the underlying paganism, but the above mentioned Christianization shows how utterly forlorn the Jews' position was, thus surrounded by their enemies: the king, the people and the clergy, for, as already said, they were an additional object of clerical trouble, especially as the Church had to admit that they were the people of God. Hence its eagerness to convert them and its bitter hatred when it failed in its attempts at conversion. And ever constant was the Church in its hatred. Richard of

[1] Joseph Jacobs, *Jewish Quarterly Review*, Vol. IV, p. 629.
[2] "Even such a simple thing as taking a farm involved paying homage, which was again connected with a religious formula". Joseph Jacobs, *Jewish Quarterly Review*, Vol. IV, p. 629.

Devizes, a monk, wrote a contemporary history of king Richard I, in which the persecutions of the Jews in particular, are described with a terrible faithfulness, which reflects the author's own avowed hatred of the race [1].

The history of the events preceding the loss of Normandy is the history of wrongs inflicted and sustained by various tribes, which indeed all dwelt on English ground, but which regarded each other with aversion such as has scarcely ever existed between communities separated by physical barriers, but before the end of the reign of Edward the Second the distinction between Norman and Saxon had almost disappeared. From this amalgamation the Jew was not only excluded, but he experienced all the disadvantages arising from the union of his enemies. Unity makes force and that force was employed against the Jews. They had brought capital, trade and industry to England. The English had learned their ways and manners and began to see them as competitors rather than as teachers, which in fact they were. Now the clergy was invited to assist the English capitalists in ousting the Jew from the market, an enterprise in which the King, still profiting by his presence, did not join.

Therefore Stephen Langton, archbishop of Canterbury, decreed several measures to suppress the Jews, some of which are interesting from a literary point of view. One prevented the mixture of Jewish men and women with Christians of each sex. The Jews of both sexes, another measure commands, have to wear a linen cloth two inches broad and four fingers long, of a dif-

[1] See also Graez, *Hist. of the Jews*, who quotes William of Newbury and Radulph de Dicedo.

ferent colour from their own clothes, on their upper garment, on their breast. Then there were measures of an economical nature. Thus we learn that the cruelty of the bishops was extraordinarily inhuman and vied with the King's: they forbade the people to sell them victuals, so that many actually perished with hunger. Monks travelled the country to preach against the Jews; the religious revival due to the Franciscans caused the worsening of the conditions of the Jews.

Strange to say there is evidence that in spite of the attempts to crush the Jews there were signs that they attracted conversion, there were instances of Christians becoming Jews, which did not mollify the feelings against them. This Jewish proselytism was met by the Church by establishing a conversionist establishment in "New Street" where converts were supported for life. This establishment continued to exist down to the time of Charles II, a fact which must not be lost sight of, for we shall have to refer to it, when dealing with literature after 1290.

Usury. — In connection with the clergy I wish to draw attention to a curious fact. We have already seen that the Christian kings did not shrink from sweating the Jew and enjoying his evil gains. A worse thing takes place with the clergy. The Canon Law forbids the loan of money on interest by any under its ecclesiastical jurisdiction, a law which practically yields the monopoly of doing so to the Jews, not from any economical motive but from a religious one. Usury was a sin and the Christian had to be kept free from it. But usury was the capitalism of that period and without capitalism there could be no progress, so this lucrative sin was grudgingly left to the hated Jew, who was thus able to maintain his ground.

But capital means power, and lucre and power were
two baits too mighty to be resisted by the clergy in the
long run and we soon see a mighty competitor crop up
in nobody less than the Pope himself, for he indeed, was
wont to carry on that infamous trade, in such a shame-
ful manner, by the help of several Italian merchants,
called Caursini, that the Jews themselves might have
profited by his example. The remarks upon the bonds
of these usurers by Matthew Paris himself are sufficient,
for when the Jews, says he, came to understand this
Christian way of preventing usury they laughed very
heartily. For preventing of usury it was hypocritically
called. Coulton in *Social Life in Britain from the Conquest to the Reformation*, page 342, translates Matthew
Paris, who tells us about the abominable Usurers of
Cahors and other towns in the South of France and North
of Italy who were infinitely more exacting than the
Jews. "Yet now the Lord Pope's merchants or money-
changers practise their usury publicly in London, to
the disgust of the Jews". Then follows an example of
their tricks and Matthew says, "This is worse than a
Jew's condition, for the Jew will receive the principal
courteously whensoever thou shalt return it, with only
so much interest as is proportionate to the time for
which thou hast it in hand". So here we have a certain
proof that the Jew as a usurer was a moderate man and
not the cruel extortioner that Literature has made of him.

So after the clergy had conquered their scruples about
usury there was little left for the poor Jew. There was
still a straw left to which the drowning fellow held fast.
As a physician he feared little as yet of Christian competition, but here too the Church found ways and means

to cut him off and simply forbade Christians to be cured by them: they had better die she said, and afterwards she forbade the Jews to practise medicine altogether, adding insult to injury by declaring them to be sorcerers.

The Jew and the People. — As for the people, I have already hinted here and there at their attitude towards the Jews. All that the clergy pleased to say about them was implicitly believed, and to religious reasons for hatred economical motives were added. As a usurer he was a capitalist and capitalists have ever been hated by non-capitalists. But in every respect they had learned practically all that the Jew could teach and in all respects the Jew found competitors among the Christians, even in usury. He had indeed become a nuisance now and his successors, the new Christian capitalists, assisted by the clergy moved the whole nation against him. The lower ranks of the people saw in him only an instrument of taxation for the benefit of the King. As I have already said, the influence of the clergy on the people was unlimited. According to the feudal principle citizenship involved spiritual communion. The guilds were on a religious basis, so at last the Jews were excluded from everything, and we may wind up by saying that the history of the Jews in England from Richard the First down to their expulsion is a series of bitter persecutions prompted by fanatic hatred in the first place and by covetousness, rapacity and ignorance on the side of the prosecutors: the clergy, the king and the people. It is only a farce, when we come across an instance of protection against the popular hatred, for then they were left to the tender mercies of their would-be protectors and this generally meant new levies of money entailing new draining of the people and thus the Jews were landed in a vicious circle.

The Blood-Sacrifice. — To the purely economical reasons, based on Christian jealousy,[1] which finally led to the expulsion of the Jews, must be added impure and immoral ones, the calumnies brought in against them, chiefly by the church, and thus we now come to a most atrocious crime of which the Jews have been accused and which has been maintained against them until this very day, although it has been proved over and over again to be against the Mosaic and Rabbinical laws as well as against all human feeling, the charge of crucifying[2] or otherwise murdering Christian children for the sake of using their blood for some religious rites, the charge of blood-sacrifice.

The first instance of this accusation we find in the Saxon Chronicle in an account of the year 1137. Toovey, whom we cannot exactly call a philo-semite, remarks that the reader will observe that the Jews are never said to have practiced it, but at such times as the king was manifestly in great want of money. To which I add that the supposed cases of crucifixion took place at times which were characterized by a religious revival, two circumstances that make me suspect that these cases were simply concocted, or if not concocted, then at any rate a crime had been committed of which the Jews were perfectly innocent, but which was eagerly made use of by the the King and the clergy; by the former to rob the Jews, by the latter to show the

[1] Barabas says that he is only hated for his happiness, the result of his successful trading.

[2] Marlowe, *Jew of Malta*. Friar Jac: "What has he crucified a child?" (end of the third act).

credulous Christian that the Jews had not yet got rid of their New Testamental propensity to crucify and that, as they. could not lay hold of Jesus himself, they took a being next to him in innocence, a young child. The people believed it and had an extra holiday in punishing the Jews, the King got their money and the clergy had the excellence of their own creed confirmed and all were happy. I can do no better that quote the *Saxon Chronicle*. "Nu we willen sægen sumdel wæt belæmp on Stephnes Kinges time. On this time the Judeus of Noruuic bohton an cristen cild beforen Estren pineden him alle the ilce pining that ure Drihten was pined on lang fridæi him on rode hengen for ure Drihtines luve sythen byrieden him. Wenden they it sculde ben forholen or ure Dryhtin atywede that he was hali martyr to munckes him namen bebyried him heglice in the minstre he maked thur ure Drihten wunderlice manifældlice miracles hatte he S'Willelm." (Earle and Plummer, *Two Saxons Chronicles Parallel*.)

Such superstition need not surprise us, when about half a century later King Richard the First forbids the Jews to be present at his coronation, for fear they should bewitch him[1]. Moreover, from a story in Richard of Devizes under 1192 it would seem to have been the natural thing to charge the Jews with crucifying any missing Christian child. In 1235 an attempt at crucifying was frustrated at Norwich (Matthew Paris). In 1244 a corpse was found of a boy killed by the Jews and in 1255 the story of Hugh of Lincoln is told in the *Annals of Waverley* by a contemporary writer. As we find a graphic description of this case in Matthew Paris, I will quote this author.

[1] Toovey.

"Et convenientes constituerunt unum Judæum Lin-
colniensem pro judice, tam quam pro Pilato, cujus judicio
et omnium favore affectus est puer diversis tormentis.

Verberatus est usque ad cruorem et livorem, spinis
coronatus, sputis et cachinis lacessitus, et insuper a
singulis punctus cultellis, qui dicuntur anelacii, potatus
felle, derisus probris et blasfemis, et crebro ab eisdem
fredentibus dentibus, Jesu pseudoprophet vocatus. Et
postquam diversimode illuserant ei, crucifixerunt et
lancea ad cor pupugerunt". This was again accompanied
by miracles.

A complete story of Hugh of Lincoln and an interesting reconstruction of the case as it probably happened
in reality, is to be found in the Transactions of the Jewish Historical Society and interesting information is found
in Toovey as well. Two earlier instances are those of 1160
at Gloucester and of 1162 at St. Edmundsbury at Easter[1].
In 1255 many Jews were executed on this charge.

So we have seen that the chief reason of the admission
of the Jews into the country was not an ideal recog-
nition of man's right to choose a place of abode where
he pleases, hoping to find a spot where he can live in
peace, security and affluence. Far from it. It was not
for his own sake that the Jew was admitted, but for
the sake of William the Conqueror. The Jew's history
down to his expulsion is a financial experiment which
the Norman King started[2]. In the Norman and Angevin
periods the Jews formed a body closely connected with
the Government and constituting an integral part of its

[1] *Transactions of the Jewish Historical Society of England*, Vol. I—II, p. 95 and
the *Jewish Encyclopaedia*.
[2] J. Jacobs & L. Wolf, *Catalogue of the Anglo-Jewish Historical Exhibition*.

financial system. The Jew was the milch-cow, the royal milch-cow and in the first period after its acquisition some special care was taken that the beast was not ill-treated and given sufficient opportunity to graze. But the combined forces of blind religious zeal and mis-understood economical interests, proved to be stronger than the king's love of money and in 1920 the Jews were driven from England. The following is an account of this calamity given by Green.

The Expulsion. — "The next year saw a step which re-mains the great blot upon Edward's reign. Under the Angevins the popular hatred of the Jews had grown rapidly in intensity. But the royal protection had never wavered. Richard had punished heavily a massacre of the Jews at York, John suffered none to plunder them save himself, though he once wrested from them a sum equal to a year's revenue of his realm. The troubles of the next reign brought in a harvest greater than even the royal greed could reap; the Jews grew wealthy enough to acquire estates, and only a burst af popular feeling prevented a legal decision which would have enabled them to own freeholds. Their pride and contempt of the superstitions around them broke out in the taunts they levelled at processions as they passed their Jewries, sometimes as at Oxford in actual attacks upon them. Wild stories floated about among the people of children carried off to Jewish houses, to be circumcised or cru-cified, and a boy of Lincoln who was found slain in a Jewish house was canonized by popular reverence as "St. Hugh." The first work of the Friars was to settle in the Hebrew quarters and attempt their conversion, (the reader should, however, bear in mind that the re-

ligious revival due to the Franciscans caused the worsening of the condition of the Jews, M.) but the tide of
popular fury rose too fast for these gentler means of reconciliation. The sack of Jewry after Jewry was the
sign of popular hatred during the Barons' war. With
its close, fell on the Jews the more terrible persecution
of the law. Statute after statute hemmed them in. They
were forbidden to hold real property, to employ Christian servants, to move through the streets without the
two white tablets of wool on their breasts, which distinguished their race. They were prohibited from building new synagogues, or eating with Christians, or acting
as physicians to them. Their trade, already crippled by
the rivalry of the bankers of Cahors, was annihilated
by a royal order, which bade them renounce usury
under pain of death. At last persecution could do no more,
and on the eve of his struggle with Scotland, Edward,
eager at the moment to find supplies for his treasury,
and himself swayed by the fanaticism of his subjects,
bought the grant of a fifteenth from the clergy and laity
by consenting to drive the Jews from his realm. Of
the sixteen thousand who preferred exile to apostasy
few reached the shores of France. Many were wrecked,
others robbed and flung overboard. One shipmaster
turned out a crew of wealthy merchants on to a sand-
bank, and bade them call a new Moses to save them
from the sea. From the time of Edward to that of
Cromwell no Jew touched English ground." [1]

The partnership is dissolved. It was an odd mixture
of a limited and unlimited liability company. The King

[1] See, however, Lee's article 'The Original of Shylock' in the Gentleman's
Magazine.

had no liability at all and the Jew's liability did never end. Let us inspect the balance sheet. The Kings had gained heaps of money, a people that thad learned trade, industry, finance, architecture, science (physic and astronomy) and the Jews had gained: exile or death, mutilation, bereavement of kith and kin, humiliation and mortification and an empty purse. And it was the pure Jew, the religious Jew, the staunch Jew, the faithful Jew who was driven out, and not the usurer, and not the incarnation of the deadly sins, and not the corrupter of good morals or the schismatic for these flourished in England as before and many a one noticed that Christians were far better hands at these practices than the Jews had been said to be.

I cannot leave Green's statement, that from the time of Edward to that of Cromwell no Jew touched English ground, unqualified. First of all history has taught us, that Jews were always exempted from the inflictions bestowed upon their more faithful brethren, if they renounced their religion. That I found no existant records of this in England does not wholly prove that this was not the case there [1]. Then I have already mentioned the conversionist establishment in 'New Street'. In addition to this we find records down to 1625 that prove that Jews did touch English ground [2]. Thus for instance we find that when Henry IV was ill in 1406, the native physicians were baffled. In his young days he had wandered a good deal over Europe, when he was still Henry of Derby and he

---

[1] In fact Green's statement that "of the 16000 who preferred exile to apostasy few reached the shores of France", I infer that there were those who preferred apostasy.
[2] We find in the 14th century that many professing to be Italians were in reality Jews, *Transactions of the Jewish Historical Soc.*, I—II., p. 5 and *Rotuli Parliamentarum* 1376, II. 332 a.

had dealt with Jews and learned of their fame as Doctors. In his need he called for one Doctor Elias Sabat the Hebrew from Bologna, who came with a retinue including ten servants with their horses and harness. Henry allowed them to remain in England for two years. As the king did not recover, he called for Doctor David di Nigarelli of Luca in Italy, who remained in England till 1412. In 1409 Alice, the daughter of Sir Ivo Fitzwarren wife to Richard Whittington (Dick Whittington of the well-known nursery tale) required permission to import a "destitute alien", Maistre Sampson de Mierbeawe judeus from the South of France, for one year to act as a physician to her.[1] In 1492 the great expulsion from Spain took place, and it seems that a number found shelter in England, for in 1493 Jewish fugitives sued a Spanish merchant in London.[2] In Speed's History an account is given of Perkin Warbeck from which we derive the following. "This youth was born they say in the city of Torney and called Peter Warbeck the son of a converted Jew, whose godfather at baptism king Edward IV himself was". The subject is dealt with by Bernard André, the court chronicler to Henry VII, as follows. "They pretended that Peter, a native of Tournai, who had been brought up thereabouts by one Edward, once a Jew, but afterwards laved in the sacred font by king Edward, was the younger son of Edward IV". This Jew has been indentified by Mr. Cecil Roth[3] with one Sir Edward Brampton (about 1468) alias Edward Brandon.

[1] Jewish Quarterly Review XVIII p. 141, A. Weiner, *A note on Jewish Doctors in England in the reign of King Henry IV.*

[2] *Transactions Jewish Hist. Society in England*, Vol 1—11 p. 55.

[3] *Transactions Jewish Hist. Society*, Vol 1X.

I quite agree with Mr. Roth, and even Mr. J. L. Cardozo, who diligently tries in his fine dissertation *The Contemporary Jew in the Elizabethan Drama* to prove the absence of Jews, only dissents from his conclusion as to the presence of other Jews.

In the sixteenth century we find further facts that prove the existence of a Marrano colony in London and in a tract written between 1600 an 1625 we find expressly stated, that "a store of Jewes we have in England; a few in court; many i' the City, more in the country" [1]. In *The Original of Shylock*, Lee gives a full biography of Dr. Lopez, the converted Jewish physician of Queen Elizabeth. See also page 166.

I am not going to conclude from the above that England teemed with Jews between 1290 and 1654, but it would be equally exaggerated to maintain that their number was so small that they escaped notice.

The Black Death and its Cause. — Having dealt with the Jew after 1290 in England, I must make mention of a calamity that curiously influenced the Jew in English Literature. As we have already shown, the Jew had to pay dearly for the fact that he differed from his fellow creatures. He was made the scapegoat of the Christians in the Middle Ages, who thought to send him to perdition laden with sin in order to become white as snow with innocence themselves. In illustration of this assertion the following may serve, which brings us to a new accusation against the Jews, namely the charge of poisoning wells, the charge of wholesale slaughter, a worthy superlative to the occasional murdering of a Christian child. On page six of *Shakespeare and the*

[1] T. Boas, *Shakespere and his Predecessors*, p. 216.

Jew by G. Friedlander we read: "When a plague arose, such as the great pestilence in France in 1320, or the Black Death in 1348—1349, it was of course the fault of the Jews. They must have poisoned the wells, (see Tross, *Westphalia*, p. 217, and Schilter in *Koeningshoven Chronik*, pp. 1021 ff.). In their thousands aye, tens of thousands, the Jews, young and old, men, women, and infants, were doomed [1].

The Jew, a Mixture of Historical Facts & Biblical Fancy. — I have spoken of the prejudices based upon the Gospel and their influence on Anglo-Saxon literature. The Normans held the same prejudices founded on the same basis, so Anglo-Saxons and Normans coalesced in their opinion about the character of the Jew. The character of the Jew was there before the Jew proper put in an appearance. That this character had really nothing in common with the true spirit of the Jew, did not prevent the English from seeing in him all the same, when he came in propria persona. The literary products we are going to discuss, will constantly bear the stamp of a peculiar mixture of fact and fancy. Literature after the Settlement reflects the Jew partly as the authors knew him from experience on account of his stay among them, partly as they had been used to consider him until then. As for their observations whilst the Jew was among them, I must start by making the sweeping assertion, that their opinions about the Jew based on his actual presence, touch only outward appearances and never go below the surface. Never did they attempt to pene-

---

[1] In John of Trevisa's version of Ralph Higden's *Polychronicon* (Rolls Series), VI. 385, we find that "in 1387 Charles Grossus was i-poysond of a Jew".

trate into the inner motives of the Jew, into his soul, never did they see him as a lover, a son, a brother, and this for two very good reasons. They were sure they knew the truth about him already in the first place, and in the second place such an attempt would only be possible after ages of civilization and they were simply not ripe for it. Hence the Jew in early English literature is a creature partly based on superficial contemporary observation, partly on traditional prejudice. His doings are partly historical, his psyche entirely fiction. This duality of construction has led many a scholar on a wrong track. Some have denied his genuineness on account of his false psychology, others again have asserted his reality on account of his superficial resemblance to a Jew proper.

The Jews' Ubiquity in Literature. — Leaving aside works on history, where the Jews are mentioned as a matter of course, the reader will perhaps be surprised to learn that there is no department of literature, where we do not find at least something about the Jew. We have already dealt with Anglo-Saxon literature and shall now find him in miscellaneous prose and poetry, in the Ballads, in the Mystery, Miracle, Morality, Interlude and practically in all stages of the Regular Drama.

William Langland's Piers Plowman. — Before entering upon an enumeration of literary products breathing a bitter spirit of intolerant prejudice, I am happy to mention an allusion in the *Vision of Piers Plowman* by William Langland [1], which can be fairly termed sympathetic. The poet prophesies a time when there shall be such a 'pees' among the people and a 'perfit

[1] *Early English Text Society,* Part III, p. 67, 1873.

trewthe' that 'Jewes shall wene in her witte and waxen
wonder glade, that Moises or Messie be come into this
erthe, and have wonder in here hertis, that men beth
so trewe' and gives a few more instances of a tolerant
spirit. Of Jewish charity Langland was bold enough
to say, for bold it was to ascribe any good quality to
the Jews, "Allas that a Cristine creature shal be un-
kynde til an other. Sitthen Jewes that we jugge Judas
felawes ayther of hem helpeth other of that hym
nedeth." [1]

The Miracles of Our Lady in the Vernon MS. We
may now take leave of this mild spirit and plunge
into the atmosphere created by the Gospel. We shall
first see a Jew wicked, murderous, hateful to God,
without natural affection. He occurs in one out of the
nine miracles of our Lady in the Vernon MS [2]. A Jew's
child, a boy, who was wont to play with Christian
children, went with the Christians to mass at Easter-
time. He knelt and prayed to the image of the Virgin
and the Child. His father saw him come from the church
and cast him into an oven. The mother raised the citizens, who found the boy in the oven unharmed. The
boy declared that, through the Virgin and her Infant,
the coals were as sweet as flowers and spices beneath
him. The mother and all the Jews were converted and
the father condemned to the oven. Another miracle tells
us how our Lady becomes surety for a merchant and
shows us the dishonesty of the Jews in money matters,
thus illustrating the Gospel where he is called covetous

---

[1] *Early English Text Society*, Part II, p. 136, 1869.
[2] R. W. Tryon in *Publications of the Mod. Lang. Association of America*, Vol.
XXXVIII, No. 2, pp. 336/337.

and deceitful. Of this story there is also a second English version [1]. Particularly rich in versions is the story of Hugh of Lincoln, which besides occurring in the sources mentioned already, is also told in the *Annals of Waverly* under 1255 and which according to F. J. Child, in his *English and Scottish Popular Ballads*, appears in twenty-one versions of a ballad entitled *Sir Hugh or The Jew's Daughter*. I mention it here because the story also occurs in the *Miracles of our Lady*, where a Jew of Paris does the cruel deed. This may have been the source of Chaucer's *Prioresses Tale*, where the story is told in the following manner.

Chaucer's Prioressess Tale. — In a great city in Asia there was a Jewry among Christian people. This Jewry was sustained by a Lord of that country for foul usury and lucre. Near this Jewry was a school, which was attended by a little boy of seven, the son of a widow. He had to pass the Jewry twice a day and as he passed he sang "Alma Redemptoris" in honour of the Holy Virgin. Of course he did not do this to spite the Jews, but only prompted by his love of the Mother of God. The devil, whose habitation is the Jew's heart, instigated the cursed Jews to have the child murdered. One of them cut his little throat and threw him into a pit, where these Jews purged their entrails. As the boy did not come home that night, the widow went to look for him and when she came to the pit, a miracle took place, for the boy, who lay there with his throat cut, began to sing "Alma Redemptoris". A crowd collected, the Provost was called and he immediately caused the Jews to be bound,

[1] A similar miracle occurs in John of Garland's *Liber Metricus*, fol. 19, col. 2.

tormented, drawn with wild horses and hanged. At
the end of the poem the murder of Hugh of Lincoln is
mentioned as a similar instance of Jewish cruelty.
Note that Chaucer thus thinks that Hugh had his
throat cut, but Matthew Paris says distinctly that he
was crucified, which must not be overlooked, for the
Christian wanted to perpetuate the crucifixion of
the Lord. As to the punishment inflicted on the Jew
into whose house Hugh of Lincoln had gone to play,
we find that he was dragged, tied to a horse's tail,
to the gallows, thus tallying pretty well with Chaucer's
tale.

When compelled by historical and logical consider-
ations, I pronounce such and similar accusations of
childmurder as perfectly groundless and results of the
ancient prejudices, I am backed by many eminent
clergymen. Thus for instance Bishop Th. Percy, in
discussing the same subject with reference to *The Ballad
of the Jew's Daughter* [1], says that "this ballad is
founded upon the supposed practice of the Jews in
crucifying or otherwise murdering Christian children,
out of hatred to the religion of their parents: a practice
which hath been always alleged in excuse for the
cruelties exercised upon that wretched people, but
which probably never happened in a single instance.
For if we consider, on the one hand, the ignorance and
superstition of the times when such stories took their
rise, the virulent prejudices of the monks who record
them, and the eagerness with which they would be
catched up by the barbarous populace as a pretence
for plunder; on the other hand the great danger

[1] *Reliques of Ancient English Poetry*, Tauchnitz Edition, Vol. I, page 32.

incurred by the perpetrators, and the inadequate motives they could have to excite them to a crime of so much horror, we may reasonably conclude the whole charge to be groundless and malicious".

A Disputation between a Christian and a Jew. — There occurs also in the Vernon MS. "A disputisoun [1] bytwene a cristenemon and a jew" which shows us a Jew in religious matters. It is a disputation between a Christian and a Jew on theological problems. Such disputations were far from rare in the Middle Ages and far from innocent, for the fate of the Jews often depended on their issue. William Rufus, for instance appointed such a public debate in London and profanely swore by "the face of St. Luke" that if the Rabbins defeated the Bishops, he would turn Jew himself. In Henry the Third's time those disputations were forbidden [2], probably because the issue was not always, as the clergy desired. The Jew in the 'disputisoun' sticks to the Mosaic Law and denies that Christ is the son of God and so far reflects the Jews' adherence to their creed. The disputants come across the crucified image of Jesus and blood begins to flow from the wounds of the Saviour and turns Saulus into Paulus. Now this was a Jew after the Christian author's heart, so he is not afraid of praising him for the very same thing for which he is generally abused in literature, his staunch adherence to his religion. "The tother was a jeuȝ riht / A mon muchel of his miht; / To his trouthe hedde he tiht / Trewe as the tre / that wol I

[1] These disputations served to break the Jews' obstinacy and promote their conversion, but at the same time to enhance the prestige of the Church.
[2] Milman, *Hist. of the Jews*, Vol. III, p. 230.

apertly preve: / thulke lay that he on levve, / For no gold that (me) mihte him geve / chaunge wolde not he".

The Pound of Flesh Incident. — Besides the accusation of poisoning wells, the Black Death had a curious influence upon the famous, or rather infamous 'pound of flesh incident', which was current in literature before it appeared in *The Merchant of Venice.* The oldest European version of the story of the Pound of Flesh is to be found in Dolopathos or *The King and the Seven Sages.* This work was composed by a trouvère, named Herbers, in the 13th century. This French metrical version is based on an old Latin manuscript of a Cistercian monk, Johannes de Alta Silva. The monk wrote his book between 1184 and 1212 (See Goedeke in *Orient und Occident,* Vol. III, p. 395).

In this and in other sources [1] the person demanding the pound of flesh i s n o J e w. He is either spoken of without any reference to some religion, or he is a heathen, or a Christian. It is strange but true that in *The Life of Pope Sixtus V,* translated from the Italian of Greg. Leti, by the Rev. Mr. E. Farneworth, where this incident also occurs, the v i c t i m is a Jew (See Percy's Reliques, *Gernutus the Jew of Venice* and Friedlander, page 15). "The Florentine novelist, swayed by the lying tales which spoke of the Jews as the authors of the Black Death, made the cruel money-lender, for the first time, a Jew" [2]. This Florentine novelist was Ser Giovanni Fiorentino, the author of *Il Pecorone,* written about 1378, which must be regarded

[1] Persian, Egyptian (*The Autobiography of Lutfullah,* Chapt. V, ed. Eastwick), Latin (*Gesta Romanorum,* p. 130, ed. Madden).
[2] G. Friedlander, *Shakespeare and the Jew,* p. 54.

as Shakespeare's main source for Shylock. Once connected with Judaism, the cruel creditor never got rid of his religious confession.

Cursor Mundi. — The story of the pound of flesh next appears in the *Cursor Mundi*[1] about the end of the 14th century. A covetous, hard-hearted Jew succeeds in persuading a Christian, who finds himself short of money, to pledge the flesh of his own body. Should part of the money not be forthcoming on the due date, then an equal part of his flesh would be cut off to make up the balance. The day of settlement arrives and the Christian fails to meet his engagement. The Christian stands empty-handed and the Jew driven by revenge and bloodthirstiness wants to torture him within an inch of his life. As soon as a signal is given by the Judge, the Jew is going to deprive his victim of his eyes, nose, nay even his tongue, with his sharp knife and does not intend to stop, till he has fulfilled his bond. But his plans are frustrated in the well-known way and the Jew "was dempt sua that the quene / sulde have his catel all bidene, / In hir merci his tung to take, / that in hir curt sli missau make". When hearing this "the iuu him thoght selcuthli tene / at this dome that was sua kene, / And said on hij, all might here, / Me war lever ʒu for to lere / Quar lijs ʒur laverd rode-tre / than dampned sua sone to be" and to crown his atonement he said so that all could hear it "Christ thou art the saviour of all this world".

So, rather than lose his possessions, this Jew forswears his Judaism. This means that the Jewish peculiarities

---

[1] *Cursor Mundi*, ed. by R. Morris, E. E. T. S., original series, 66—68, Part V, pp. 1226—1232.

disappear as if by magic by turning Christian. These peculiarities are not inherent, consequently they are only the outcome of his Jewish religion, which must therefore be a complete guidance for rascals, an absurd notion which was not uncommon in the Middle Ages.

John Gower's Confessio Amantis. — The true New Testament Jew is met again in John Gower's *Confessio Amantis*[1]. As in the Vernon MS., he is a liar, a swindler, a thief. The story is like this. A Jew and a heathen are travelling in the same direction. The heathen rides upon a donkey which is heavily burdened, the Jew travels on foot. In the course of their conversation they speak about their ethical principles. The heathen pleads for loving one's neighbour and considers benevolence, pity, compassion and charity as sovereign virtues. The Jew, however, openly admits that he does not know the love of truth and is not troubled by breaking the commandment "thou shalt not steal". "I am a Jew, and bi mi lawe / I shal to no man be felawe / To kepe him trcwthe in word ne dede, / Bot if he be withoute drede / A verrai Jew as am I, / For elles I mai trewely / Bereve him bothe lif and good." All right, says the sly Jew at the end of the conversation, practise what you preach and pity the man who has to walk in the scorching sun, give me your donkey. The heathen complies with his request, but getting exhausted claims his beast again. The Jew, however, gallops away with it and with the burden it carries. Deviating from his original [2], John Gower thought

[1] *The Complete Works of John Gower*, by G. C. Macaulay, Oxford 1901, Vol. 3, p. 321.

[2] *Secretum Secretorum*, printed in Gower's EnglishWorks, ed. by G. C. Macaulay, Vol. II, pp. 320—322.

it necessary to make a lion tear the Jew to pieces.

Romances. Titus and Vespasian. — In the Romances too the Jew as we know him from the New Testament is present. Between 1450—1475 we find histories in the form of romances in which the story of the New Testament is taken for subject matter, to which must be added *Titus and Vespasian or the Destruction of Jerusalem*. (I may as well add that Titus and Vespasion are often looked upon as instruments in the hand of God to avenge the crucifixion of the Saviour).

Anth. Munday, Of a Jew who would for his Debt have a Pound of the Flesh of a Christian. — Before Shakespeare we once more meet the 'pound of flesh story' about 1591, when Anthony Munday wrote '*Of a Jew who would for his debt have a pound of the flesh of a Christian*'. 'This is a translation from the French of the 95th declamation in the '*Orator*' of Alexander Silvayn and Shylock's speech in the court may possibly have been suggested by it. It is printed at full length in the Variorum editions of Shakespeare.

The Ballads. — All things considered the Jew must have been a subject eminently fit for ballads or folk-songs and no doubt he was used as such. Ballads had been sung in England from very early times, they had travelled over the whole country among the people. A crowd of minstrels sang them through city and village. I think I am not far wrong in supposing that there must have been a good many ballads with the Jew for subject, which have got lost. I have been looking for some ancient ones that might illustrate my subject and I think I have succeeded in finding a small number that bear out my assertion.

Judas. — There is in the first place the 13th century ballad of Judas. On the whole it is the same Judas of the Gospel. We must of course expect some modification. Thus, for instance, we find the addition to his story of a sister, a false Jewess, and a motive for the selling of Christ to the Jews, namely a desire of Judas to reimburse himself for thirty pieces of silver of which he had been robbed [1]. No doubt this was one of a series of religious folk songs which all told the story of some interesting personality good or bad, taken from the Old or New Testament or the Lives of Saints.

St. Stephen and Herod. — About 1450 there is the ballad of St. Stephen and Herod demonstrating the Jew's cruelty.

The Harrowing of Hell. — I should perhaps first have mentioned a curious production, which is considered by some as one of the oldest ballads, by others as one of the earliest attempts at dramatic writing and based on the apocryphical gospel of Nicodemus, called *The Harrowing of Hell.* It contains indeed some elements of the drama and is assigned to the early part of the 14th century. This interesting piece is introduced by a prologue the beginning of which reminds one of a ballad "Alle herkneth to me nou, a strif will I tellen ou, of Jesu and of Satan". Christ and Satan interchange some half score speeches of summons and refusal; the janitor runs away, and the Lord, binding Satan, is welcomed by the patriarchs and graciously answers them in turn. I feel sorely tempted to quote the whole Harrowing of Hell in illustration of what I have said about Jesus and Satan as replacing the old pagan

[1] F. J. Child's *English and Scottish Popular Ballads.*

heroes and their enemies, and about the position of the Jews of the Old Testament. Adam and Eve, Abraham, David and Moses are saved and have become Christians to all intents and purposes, curious instances of conversion, a thing the Christians have ever strenuously striven after. The theme remained a much favoured one for quite a long time and logically follows from the fact that the Old Testament Jews have not only been praised, but even sainted and it would not do to leave such precious souls unsaved and in the power of Satan.

Gernutus. — The Ballad of Gernutus, the forerunner of Shylock, brings us to quite another type. Here we are no longer in Palestine. Here we have not to deal with the enemy of Christ in the first place. The balladmaker mentions Italian writers as his authorities [1]. This poem contains the story of a cruel Jew, a usurer [2], who by way of a merry jest concludes a strange bond with a Christian merchant, who stands in need of a hundred crowns. The bond runs that no interest will be given or taken, but a pound of the debtor's flesh will be cut from his body, in case he should be in default. The Jew's motives are understood to be pure hate and hopes of torturing his hereditary enemy and for this purpose he is prepared to forego his profits and even a hundred thousand crowns that are offered, when later on the Christian really cannot meet his obligations. The Jew is preparing for the cruel deed, he whets his knife, but has reckoned without his host. The Judge, before

[1] Percy's *Reliques*. The original is in the Pepysian Library, Magdalen College, Cambridge.
[2] In a ballad in Rollins' collection *A Pepysian Garland* all Jews are called Usurers, p. 188.

whom the case has been brought, proves to be a second
Solomon, forbids the shedding of even a drop of Christian blood, as this has not been stipulated. The Jew is
defeated and does not receive a penny. We have
seen that in the source of the Pound-of-Flesh incident
the cruel one is a Christian and we know from Matthew
Paris that the Christian usurers were worse than the
Jewish ones, who were moderate and civil, so I should
not be surprised, if the whole situation was originally
meant as a satire against the Pope's usurers, who under
the pretext of lending money gratis managed to ruin
their victims completely. This ballad shows already
the dangerous duality of reality and prejudicial fancy.
For we know that the Jew was a usurer and many
may have insisted on the fulfilment of engagements
and may have been rather exacting, which is not against
human nature, but as soon as we are told about his
wickedness, maliciousness, bloodthirstiness and total
absence of mercy, we see again the uncritical, prejudicial
tradition that finds its source in the Gospel[1].

The Jew's Daughter. — Child-murder crops up again
in the ballad of *The Jew's Daughter*[2]. Why is it no
longer a Jew, why no married Jewess, but a young
female that is now guilty of the heinous crime? Was
it perhaps necessary to make the young and pretty
Jewesses hateful to Christians who were willing to
forget their duties when looking into a pair of lustrous
dark eyes? We know from history[3] that a priest was
punished for marrying a Jewish girl and we shall see

[1] We find an echo of this Ballad in the Roxburghe Ballads, Vol. I, p. 132.
[2] Th. Percy, *Reliques of Ancient English Poetry*, Tauchnitz, Vol. 1, p. 32.
[3] Toovey.

that special restrictions were laid upon women somewhat later than upon men. Whatever the reason may be, fact is that in this ballad we come across the Jew's daughter for the first time acting the principal part. Mirry-land toune (probably a corruption of Milan) on the Pa (evidently the river Po, although the Adige, not the Po, runs through Milan) is the scene of the murder. Here ten boys are at play, when the Jew's daughter arrives and by offering an apple, entices one of them to come and dine with her. At the Jew's house she kills the boy by stabbing him, lays him on a dressing-board, dresses him like a swine, laughs and tells him to go and play now with his little friends. Then she rolls him in a 'cake of lead' and drops him into a well. In this poem the boy's name is Hew, his mother's, Lady Helen. Here as in the Prioresses Tale, the mother goes to look for her son and here too the dead lad speaks out, but then the poem stops.

The Wandering Jew. — *The Wandering Jew* [1] occupies a peculiar place. It is again the story of wicked Jew of the well-known stamp: a scoffer, insolent and void of gentleness, this time in Jerusalem, who, when Christ carried his heavy cross, and, being weary, wanted to rest upon a stone, said to him "Away, thou King of Jews, thou shalt not rest here." To which the Lord replied, "I sure will rest, but thou shalt walke, and have no journey stayed", and thus it came about that this Jew has wandered up and down the world, looking precisely as he did when the Son

[1] The original story is older than 1228 (Matthew Paris), but the Jew meant in the ballad lived in Hamburg in 1547, so the ballad is of a later date (Percy's *Reliques*). See also the Roxburghe Ballads on the Wandering Jew and the *Wandering Jew's Chronicle*, Vol. I, XXIV.

of God suffered on the cross; has wandered from place to place, tormented by the thought of his wicked deed. His repentance is without an end, and this repenting Jew is looked upon by the ballad-maker with something bordering on reverence, as if he had become a Christian. As a further investigation of ballads has opened no new vistas I conclude by saying that this branch of literature again shows us Jews of the Old Testament treated with due respect and Jews of the New Testament, enemies of the Lord, in the well-known way. The Jew of the Middle Ages differs only from the latter type by having the additional qualities of a grasping usurer.

The Religious Drama. — We have already said that although Christianity had been introduced into England, its teachings had not yet weaned its inhabitants of all the errors of heathendom. Far from it. Its advocates had a hard task in doing this work of salvation and eagerly availed themselves of every opportunity and all means. Thus we have now come to a new way of spreading the Gospel amongst those in want of instruction. Its preachers had hitherto availed themselves of the word only, now they hit upon a new manner. They would not only speak about it to the masses, they would show it and this proved to be a huge success. Their new attempts were going to give rise to the crowning glory of Literature, to the Drama through its stages of development: the Mystery, Miracle, Morality and Interlude. That the Jew would figure in it, went without saying, that he would figure in it in the way already familiar to us in Literature down to this period was a matter of course, but he would be shown with additional features based upon the composers' personal acquaintance with him, which was going to give additional zest to the dramatic representations of the Gospel.

Mysteries and Miracles. — Prof. Ward [1] says "Mysteries deal with Gospel events only, their object being primarily to set forth by illustration of the prophetic history of the Old Testament, and more particularly of the fulfilling history of the New, the central mystery of the redemption of the world ,as accomplished by the Nativity, the Passion and the Resurrection", with other words the Gospel is more or less identical in subject matter with the Mysteries. The Miracles treat the lives of Saints and are, so to say, extended Mysteries. Together they are the Christian teachings dramatized. Before the Norman Conquest we have no reason to suppose that dramatic representations were known in England [2]. The performance of the earliest play of which we have any mention must probably be assigned to the reign of William Rufus (1056—1100). According to Matthew of Paris (writing about 1240) a miracle play in honour of Saint Katharine was performed about the year 1100, while the last performance on record took place in 1595 about five centuries later. Their popularity was great and their influence upon the public mind in accordance with their popularity, hence they made of the Jew a notorious character.

We have seen from history that there were plenty of Jews in England before 1290, when 16000 who preferred exile to apostasy, left the country. So it would be rather absurd to believe that the Jew of the

[1] *Engl. Dramatic Lit.* Vol. I, p. 23.
[2] A. W. Pollard, *English Miracle Plays*, p. XVIII.

Mystery was not taken from life, and I think that there cannot be the least doubt that, whenever a Jew was represented in a Mystery or Miracle play, they imitated one from real life rather than from an other source that would not have appealed to the public so much. And of Jews there are plenty in those plays. Thus for instance they compel Jesus to bear the cross, scourge and drag Him with ropes. Another good reason for supposing that the authors took the English Jews to figure in the Mystery as the Lord's worst enemies is, that the clergy and the people hated them and wanted to make propaganda against them and what better means was there to achieve their purpose than to show the then Jew on the primitive stage. They availed themselves of this opportunity with a vengeance. In the Order of the Pageants of the Play of Corpus Christi [1], anno 1415 I found, exclusive of such Jew as Abraham, Moses, etc., some fifty of them [2].

We have no miracles dating earlier than 1290 the year of the expulsion of the Jews. But we may safely say that the tradition of two centuries (1100—1290) as to his peculiar manners and outward appearance sufficed to fix him in all details, to stereotype him for the coming three centuries, even if we had not had conclusive proofs for the uninterrupted presence of the Jews between 1290 and their official return. From the above we may conclude, that as to outward appearance and peculiar manner the Jew was handed down from the earliest Miracles, of which we have no extant examples, down to Shylock.

[1] The York Plays composed between 1340—1350, 48 in number, follow the Bible narrative very closely.

[2] A. W. Pollard, *Englisch Miracle Plays*, pages XXXI/XXXV.

I have already discussed and explained the peculiar fact that whenever Jews are dealt with as a nation or as individuals living in Palestine in Biblical times, they are never considered in the same way, as when they appear as contemporary with Jesus and as his enemies or later on in exile as strangers among the Christians. In the first case they are generally treated with some reverance or at least in a neutral way, in the second they can do no good whatever. We can trace this neutral treatment in the drama as well, starting, for instance, with the 14th century *Abraham and Isaac* down to William Heming's *The Jewes Tragedy* about three centuries later. Thus, for instance, we find no disagreeable things about them in the mystery *Jacob and Esau,* where only the names distinguish them from the ordinary Christians of the period. The same holds good for *Cain and Abel* or *Joseph* in the Townely Mysteries. We find a different state of affairs as soon as we come to the Jew of the New Testament. Do not forget that the truth about the Jews must be Gospel truth, that the liturgical play is a kind of didactic play. As for outward appearance and inferior mannerisms they may take the actual Jew, but his most important features, his traits of character *must* be the same as we find them in the epistle of Paul to the Romans. They must show unrighteousness, wickedness, covetousness, maliciousness, envy, murder, strife, deceit, malignity; they must be whisperers, backbiters, hateful to God, insolent, haughty, boastful inventors of evil things, disobedient to parents, without understanding, covenant-breakers, without natural affection and unmerciful. And this the composers of the Mystery started and the composers

of the Regular Drama finished; between them they
accomplished the task of foisting upon the world
the blackest scoundrel that ever was, and that in the
shape of a real Jew, be his name Herod or Shylock.
Let us select a few characters in illustration of my
assertion and let us start with the Jew Herod. Before
doing so I will draw attention to an obvious fact, the
propagandists of the Gospel would have done their
work badly, if in the first place they had chosen
Jews of whom history has recorded a good character
and if they had gifted him with the historically good
characteristics of the Jews. They have mostly shown
bad Jews and bad or at any rate not precisely good
qualities, both based upon fact, and infused their
characters further with the imaginary qualities of the
Gospel.

Gesticulation. — Thus for instance Herod was a bad
Jew, even from the point of view of the Jews themselves, but whether this justifies that he is represented
as a wildly gesticulating Jew is an open question. That
gesticulation is a habit of Jews is not altogether wrong,
and based upon fact, but it is altogether wrong to
make all Jews gesticulate, and degenerate that gesticulation into grimaces and wild movements, and then to
make a Jewish King indulge in this, is grotesque
exaggeration. Gesticulation in a refined manner may
be a very elegant thing.

Jargon. — That many Jews spoke bad English was
probably true, as great numbers came at various
times from the continent, but no doubt there will
have been excellent linguists among those who had
lived long enough in one country. Does this justify

to make all Jews speak a sort of jargon and to make a
Jewish King be guilty of it? Once for all, if a Jew
spoke a broken tongue, it did not imply that he was
inferior in speaking-powers to a native, only that
he knew an other language besides his own and that
he did not speak that second language to perfection.

Wroth, Bragging and Cruelty. — St. Matthew says
Herod's wroth when he saw that he had been deceived
was exceedingly great and this wroth can be traced
wherever Herod comes upon the stage. His bluster has
given rise to the expression 'to outherod Herod.' He
is identified with cruelty and the prototype of the
stage villain. His bragging echoes through the drama.
In the York-series of Mysteries, Ward says, preserved
in a 15th century MS. we find that [1] tyrants,
especially and the enemies of our Lord, are depicted
with powerful realism. Annas, for example, shows a
grim joy at holding the defenceless victim in his
power, but then falls into a violent passion at what
he takes to be that victim's obduracy; he says, "we might
as wele talke tille a tome tonne", he even attempts to
strike Jesus, but Caiaphas holds him back. But above
all the figure of Judas is represented in a way more
dramatic and more impressive than in any other
medieval mystery, both in the scene where he offers
his services as betrayer, and in another where, in an
agony of remorse, he implores the high priest to take
back the money and spare Jesus. He is coldly refused,
and, when he grows more and more violent and
importunate, Caiaphas bids him be off, or he will
be taught how to behave to his betters. This Judas

[1] *The Cambridge History of English Literature*, 1918, Vol. V, Part I, p. 46.

bequeathed to the Jew not only his villainous treachery, his distinguishing inner trait, but also a distinguishing outer feature, his red beard, which was handed down (figuratively) to Shylock. Besides these prominent Jews and the Caiphas of a mystery-play of that name of the early part of the 14th century [1] there are a great many more: Pharisees, Sadducees and Scribes. The chief priests and the whole council sought false witnesses against Jesus, that they might put him to death, and the chief priests and the elders persuaded the multitudes that they should ask for Barabbas and destroy Jesus. So we see the Jew is the hostile element in the liturgical drama.

The Jew's comic Character. — It will no doubt have struck the reader that there is something grotesque in these Jews. This comical distortion and some of the absurdities were no doubt introduced on purpose to make the Jew not only detestable but also ludicrous for the benefit of the spectators, a fact which must not be overlooked, for this again has been handed down throughout the ages. No doubt even as he is now, the Jew was ridiculed then, on account of everything that distinguished him from the Christians. So we need not marvel that this was imitated on the stage and gave rise to the Jew's degradation into a comic character. Thus we find a comic intermezzo, a grotesque dance performed by the Jews, with accompaniment of music round the cross on which Christ hangs. This is to be met with not only in the Coventry Mysteries, but, likewise in some German mystery plays [2].

---

[1] *A Manual of the Writings in Middle English*, by J. E. Wells, Oxford University Press, 1916, p. 544.

[2] *The Cambridge History of English Literature*. Vol. V, pt. I, p. 44.

Nor are the Jews any better off in the miracles. *Play of Sacrament.* — Before passing on to the Moralities I shall quote Pollard on the Croxton *Play of Sacrament* of the second half of the 15th century. "The medieval hatred of the Jews gave rise to a succession of legends of their obtaining possession of the Consecrated Host, and by fire and sword endeavouring to torture afresh the Christ believed by devout worshippers to be there present. In a Yorkshire church a fresco has recently been uncovered, [1] in which is commemorated such an attempt on the part of some Flemish Jews in the fourteenth century. The Croxton play deals with a miracle 'don in the forest of Aragon. In the famous cite Eraclea, the yere of owr lord God m.cccc.lxi.' It introduces Aristorius, a Christian merchant, who for one hundred pounds procures the Host for the Jews; Ser Isoder, his chaplain; Jonathas, Jason, Jasdon, Masphat and Malchus, five Jews, of whom the first is the chief; a Bishop, and a Quack Doctor, with Colle, his servant, who are called in to heal the hand of Jonathas, withered as a result of his sacrilege" [2]. Jesus burst the building and reproached the Jews and these were converted. The play is said to be based on a French legend of about 1290.

I mentioned already the year 1595 as the year of the last Miracle-play, when Archdeacon Rogers witnessed

---

[1] For not only the stage, but art too, was used to illuminate the Bible in the Middle Ages, when reading was practically restricted to a few scholars. In art too the Jew was represented in the same way. The instance mentioned above is the only one I came across in England, but on the Continent it was quite an ordinary thing. See David Strumpf, *Die Juden in der mittelalterlichen Mysterien-, Mirakel- und Moralitäten-Dichtung Frankreichs.*

[2] A. W. Pollard, *English Miracle Plays*, Oxford, 1909, p. xliv.

one of the last performances of the Whitsun plays
at Chester the year before his death, and I say once
more that, even if we had not had conclusive proofs
of the uninterrupted presence of the Jews in England
from 1290 till 1595, Shakespeare and his contemporaries
would have had material enough to create a creature
resembling a Jew, for I venture to maintain that the
figure of the Jew, of which Shylock is one of the last
oldfashioned representatives, was quite familiar to
those dealing with the drama on account of its presence
in the Miracle and Mystery. Every man of culture or
reading or experience in Shakespeare's time had the
settled prejudicial opinion about the Jew, which with
some persons has survived even until the present
day.

The Morality. — "In its earlier days the morality
was not wholly unworthy to be ranked with the
Miracle plays, to which it formed a complement. The
Miracle play takes as its basis the historical books of
the Bible and the legends of the Church, but these
alone do not furnish a complete answer to the questions
'What must I do — What must I believe — to be
saved?' and in the two centuries during which the
popularity of the sacred drama was at its height,
various plays were written in which the moral and
sacramental teaching of the Church are assigned the
prominence which in the Miracle play is occupied by
its history" [1]. Now I ask, is it possible that during
five centuries the Jew figures in the Miracles and that
when, at a comparatively early date, a new form of
drama arises closely allied to the Miracles and forming

[1] Pollard, *English Miracle Plays*, p. xliii.

a complement to them, the Jew will suddenly and completely disappear from it? No! If the Jew represented all evil passions and sins, half the interest of the Miracle must have centred in him. If we know that in the lost play of the Lord's Prayer 'all manner of vices and sins were held up to scorn, and the virtues were held up to praise'[1], we know where we have to look for the Jew. If we know that the personified powers of good and evil, the Seven Cardinal Virtues and the Seven Deadly Sins fight for the possession of man's soul, we know what is the essence of the Morality and we know where we must look for the Jew.

St. Mary Magdalen. — Fortunately we have a play which shows the transition from Miracle or Mystery into Morality, so that we have a last glimpse of the Jew, before he hides himself behind such neutral names as Infidelity or Mammon or Vice or Devil. This is the play of *St. Mary Magdalen.* Infidelity, the Vice of the play, performs the part of Mary's lover and says of himself that at the Crucifixion time his name was *Moysaical Justice* and that he sticks so much in Jews' hearts that they will not believe the doctrine and wonders of Jesus. He is there to thwart Christ and declares himself a devil the son of the Devil. He acts the part of the Jews especially of Judas of the Mystery, for under false pretence he invites Jesus in order to entrap him. By his side, however, we have the real Jew still in Simon the Pharisee, a servile, cringing character, having all

---

[1] Once on a time a play setting forth the goodness of the Lord's Prayer was played in the city of York; in which play all manner of vices and sins were held up to scorn, and the virtues were held up to praise. *English Gilds*, by Toulmin Smith, p. 137. This play, which is lost, was the first Morality and written a century before the Castle of Perseverance, its earliest extant successor.

the qualities ascribed to the medieval Jew: a criminal
on the sly, committing his crime in such a manner as
to escape blame for lack of evidence. So we see that
the characters of an abstract or allegorical nature, intended to represent vices and passions, introduced into
the miracles at a comparatively early date, were the
successors of the Jew, who like a veritable dragon
split asunder, each part of him growing up to an independent sin or vice. When at length we come across
such characters as Reufin and Lyon partaking of
greater individuality than such vague abstractions
as Death or Pity, we have the personifications of the
feelings and passions which are supposed to have actuated the Jews against the Saviour [1]. Perhaps I had
better mention in passing that these personifications
postulated a greater necessity for distinctiveness in the
portraiture of character, which was required for the
Morality, and thus gradually led up to a figure like
Shylock. For the individuality of the characters of
the Miracle or Mystery was based either upon history
or, as in the case of the Jews, upon the prescription of
the Gospel, but not in the first place upon personal
discrimination and artisticity on the side of the com-
poser [2].

It is of course very difficult to say in a real Morality
like *Every Man* or *The Castle of Perseverance* that
this or that character is the personification of a Jewish
vice, for when once detached from the creature of
flesh and blood, I think the vice or sin looks pretty
much the same, whether it possessed a Jew or non-

[1] Keltie, *British Dramatists*, p. XXVI.
[2] For further discussion of this subject see page 168.

Jew. But no doubt the actors will have retained their Jewish peculiarities and when we meet Mammon with a long nose in a morality, we need not doubt, who is meant by this. And though I cannot prove it, I think that for False Witness and Envy the same holds good. For the latter smack too much of the Gospel and the former reflects the evil of usury. Creizenach, speaking about the Morality *Respublica* (Vol. III. p. 426), says that Avarice is the Vice of the play, and as the Jew is Avarice incarnated, I do not think it improbable that the Jew is meant here.

Devil, Vice and Jew. — In passing I have mentioned the Devil and the Vice and superficially I made a mistake in indentifying them with the Jews. As for the Vice I have already made good my assertion by referring to *Mary Magdalen*, and though the Vice says there that he is a son of the Devil, I think I had better adduce some firmer grounds for mentioning the Devil and the Jew in one breath. From the Gospel we learned already that among the supernatural enemies of the Lord, Lucifer is the foremost. Now the Jews ought to be considered as the people of God, but this would not do because the Christians wanted God for themselves, so they slyly foisted the Devil on to the Jews, so much so that in the regular drama these two are synonymous as I shall show later on.

Another thing that joins Jew and Devil is the following: like the Jew, the Devil was imported into the Morality from the old Miracle play, where again, like the Jew, he figured so amusingly. The Devil's bottle-nose and evil face are mentioned in *Like will to Like* and in *All for Money*. Like the Jew he was prone to

roaring and crying out [1]. The Devil is generally accompanied by the Vice, a fact which I do not want to
be forgotten, for when Devil and Vice appear no longer
on the stage in the regular drama, their places are
taken by the Jew and his servant. The Vice belabours
his master the Devil, the Jew is always poked fun at,
or taken in by his servant.

We shall skip the Interlude, as it does not modify
the conclusions we have arrived at and shall pass on to
the regular drama. The first play, however, that we shall
discuss has perhaps greater affinity with the Moralities
than with the regular drama, as it still contains the
characters of the older sort of play, the personifications,
a reason the more to consider it first.

The regular Drama. Wilson's Three Ladies of London.
In 1584 Robert Wilson, Shakespeare's contemporary,
wrote *The Three Ladies of London.* This play brings
to my mind the famous lines of Shelley, written among
the Euganean Hills.

> "Many a green isle needs must be
> In the deep wide sea of Misery,
> Or the mariner, worn and wan,
> Never thus could voyage on...."

The mariner, worn and wan is the Jew and the deep
wide sea of Misery is English Literature as far as the
Jew is concerned. I cannot speak of *many* a green isle
in it, but only of one, and this is the play written by
Wilson in which the Jew for the first time is accredited
with something like an ordinary human character.
Great honour is due to the author, whose keen eye

---

[1] In France the Jews were actually represented as Devils. "In Chaumont wurden
die Juden in Gestalt von Teufeln dargestellt, die sich grosse Mühe gaben, den
Eintritt der Prozession in die Stadt zu verhindern." David Strumpf, *Die Juden
in der mittelalterichen Mysterien-, Mirakel- und Moralitäten-Dichtung Frankreichs.*

discovered an error that was ages old and had become as firmly established as the Gospel itself, and greater honour is due to his brave and honest spirit that made him write down and publish his discovery. Wilson was the only man who saw and ventured to portray a Jew in a tolerant spirit. The Jew of the play, Gerontus, is represented in a very favourable light, as an upright Jew, only anxious to obtain his own property by fair means, while his antagonist, a Christian merchant, endeavours to defeat the claim by fraud, perjury and apostacy. So far the drama of the Three Ladies contradicts the position, founded mainly upon Marlowe's Barabas (in *The Jew of Malta*) and Shakespeare's Shylock, that our early dramatists eagerly availed themselves of popular prejudices against the conscientious adherents to the old dispensation.

S. Lee in *Elizabethan England and the Jews* says that this play, with its three Jewish scenes was exceptionally popular and that it was reprinted for a second time in 1592. It sometimes occurs that the Devil is given his due, but that such a thing should take place with a Jew in Literature, is a rarity that justifies a fuller description of this play. "Its dramatis personae are personifications of Fame, Love and Conscience, who do battle with personifications of Lucre, Fraud, Usury and Simony. Into this impersonal environment there is incongruously introduced one Mercatore, an Italian merchant, who speaks broken English, traffics in expensive luxuries, and is harassed by a Jewish creditor named Gerontus. Three scenes deal solely with the Jew's claim on the Italian, and they are worth the attention of the literary historian, who has persistently overlooked them." "You know", says the Jew in the first scene, "I lent you two thousand ducats for three months space, and ere the time came you got another thousand by flattery and thy smooth face; so when the time came that I should have received my money, you were not to be found, but was fled out of the country." In a second scene the Jew opens the attack thus — "Signor Mercatore, why do you not pay me? Think you I will be mocked in this sort? This three times you have flouted me, — it seems you make thereat a sport. Truly pay me my money, and that even now presently, or by mighty Mahomet (!!), I swear I will forthwith arrest thee". The merchant is obdurate, and the Jew places him under arrest. The Jew's suit is the subject of the third scene. Gerontus briefly states his complaint before "the learned Judge". Mercatore pleads that he has turned Turk (the scene passes in Turkey), and has thus, according to a recognised Turkish law, relieved himself of his debts. But while the merchant is repeating after the judge a formal renunciation of Christianity, the Jew interrupts — "stay there, most puissant judge. Signor Mercatore, consider what you do. Pay me the principal, as for the interest I forgive it you."

Merc. No point da interest; no point da principal.
Geront. Then pay me now one half, if you will not pay
(me all.
Merc. No point da half, no point denier; me will be a
Turk, I say. Me be weary of my Christ's religion.

Gerontus confesses himself shocked by the merchant's dishonest conversion, and rather than be party to it, releases him from the debt[1]. Mercatore returns to his old faith, and congratulates himself on cheating the Jew of his money. The judge adds "Jews seek to excel Christianity and Christians in Jewishness," and the episode closes.

There are, too, similarities between the dialogue of Mercatore and Gerontus and that of Antonio and Shylock, which suggest that Shakespeare knew *The Three Ladies* or the source whence its Jewish scenes were borrowed. E. Koeppel in *Konfessionelle Strömungen in d. dramat. Dichtung d. Zeitalters des beiden ersten Stuartkönige*, in *Shakespeare Jahrbuch*, Vol. XL, pp. XVI ff., also contrasts the victorious Jewish moneylender in Wilson's play with Barabas, Shylock and the villainous Jewish figures in Daborne's *A Christian turned Turk*, Day, Rowley and Wilkins' *Travailes of the Three English Brothers*, and Fletcher's *Custom of the Country*[2]. Friedlander[3] speaking of Wilson's Jew says "This is the Jew of History, to whom the crown of a 'Good Name' is supreme. He knows that it is better to be wronged than to wrong".

The Jew. -- More in keeping with the opinion in vogue at that time about the Jew is a play written before 1579. The play itself is lost, but some account of it has come down to us, for Stephen Gosson, writing in 1579, in the 'Schoole of Abuse', enumerates among the few plays which were 'tolerable at sometime', and 'without rebuke', *The Iew* and *Ptolome*, showne at the Bull, the *one* representing the greedinesse of

---

[1] This is different from Benwash's behaviour in *A Christian turned Turk*, who panders his sister-in-law to Ward to persuade the latter to become a Turk.
[2] In fact Koeppel considers the subsequent representation of Jews as a kind of reaction upon Wilson's play.
[3] *Shakespeare and the Jew.*

worldly chusers, and bloody mindes of usurers: The
other.... etc. Undoubtedly this lost play also dealt
with the pound of flesh incident and represented the
Jew as a merciless avaricious Usurer. It was a popular
play and was acted till the end of the century.

It should be noted in passing that the Jew in the
religious drama is chiefly the enemy of the Lord and
the Church and only incidentally connected with money
matters. In the regular drama, dealing with non-religious
subjects and touching social matters which were
modern from the point of view of the dramatists, things
are reversed and the Jew is in the first place the product of the Middle Ages, the usurer or merchant and in
the second place the hater of the Christians.

Marlowe's Jew of Malta. — In order to understand *The
Jew of Malta,* the drama we shall next deal with, in
order to understand the character of Barabas, the Jew
of the play, it is not sufficient to know only those
things which I have already mentioned, though they
throw much light on this drama and its Jew, the latter
being again guilty of all vices and atrocities occurring
in anteceding literature. It is equally necessary to
know something about the notorious Machiavelli,
who together with the Jew curiously influenced the
then Drama and one Joan Miquez, a Portuguese Jew,
who in his time was both known and feared in Christian
Europe as a notorious hater of Christians.

Machiavelli. — Machiavelli was born in 1469. In his
Critical and Historical Essays [1], Macaulay says of him,
"we doubt whether any name in literary history be so
generally odious as that of the man whose character

[1] Tauchnitz, 1850, Vol. I, p. 61.

and writings we now propose to consider." (Niccolo Machiavelli, a Florentine statesman, author of a work 'del Principe', in which unscrupulous statecraft is advocated). "The terms in which he is commonly described would seem to import that he was the Tempter, the Evil Principle, the discoverer of ambition and revenge, the original inventor of perjury, and that, before the publication of his fatal Prince, there had never been a hypocrite, a tyrant, or a traitor, a simulated virtue, or a convenient crime. One writer gravely assures us that Maurice of Saxony learned all his fraudulent policy from that execrable volume. Another remarks that since it was translated into Turkish, the Sultans have been more addicted than formerly to the custom of strangling their brothers. Lord Lyttelton charges the poor Florentine with the manifold treasons of the house of Guise and with the massacre of St. Bartholomew. Several authors have hinted that the Gunpowder Plot is to be primarily attributed to his doctrines, and seem to think that his effigy ought to be substituted for that of Guy Faux. The Church of Rome has pronounced his works accursed things. Nor have our own countrymen been backward in testifying their opinion of his merits. Out of his surname they have coined an epithet for a knave, and out of his Christian name a synonym for the Devil."

On page 82 Macaulay describes the character of the Italian statesman, and mentions his good qualities by the side of his bad ones. Marlowe wanted to create a Machiavellian character in the shape of a Jew, but as a product of his time Marlowe only saw and for his purpose only wanted to see the black side of such a

character. This black side according to Macaulay, and
as will be shown by me also according to Marlowe, was
the following. Among other things he was a man who
never hesitates at an oath, when he wishes to seduce,
who never wants a pretext, when he is inclined to betray.
His cruelties spring from deep and cool meditation.
His whole soul is occupied with vast and complicated
schemes of ambition. Hatred and revenge eat into his
heart, yet every look is a cordial smile, every gesture,
a familiar caress. He never excites the suspicion of his
adversaries by petty provocations. Military courage
he neither possesses nor values. With him the most
honourable means are those which are the surest, the
speediest, and the darkest He cannot comprehend how
a man should scruple to deceive those whom he does not
scruple to destroy. A traitor, hypocrite, coward and
assassin. In his wickedness he shows a strange courage,
perseverance and presence of mind. The dangers he
faces never paralyse his inventive faculties.

Sometimes reality is wilder that the wildest imagination. Napoleon towers in some respects far above
Tamburlaine and Cæsar Borgia above Barabas. In *The
Jew of Malta* wild fiction bestowed upon the Jew a
spirit which is not inferior in wickedness to the spirit
of the Devil and yet this spirit of the Jew is only a
contorted reflection of the infinitely worse spirit of a
real Christian Prince, Cæsar Borgia, and a real Christian
Statesman, Machiavelli.

Let us now pass on to Joan Miquez.

L. Kellner in *Die Quellen von Marlowe's Jew of Malta*
tells us and makes it quite acceptable that the original
of Barabas was a Portuguese Jew, one Joan Miquez or

Johannes Michesius. In his youth he had experienced the persecution of his race in Portugal, he had suffered from the Inquisition. In the twenties of the 16th century he went to Antwerp. The riches of his family were threatened by Charles the Fifth. He fled from country to country and also lived in Venice. At last he arrived at Constantinople. He had embraced the Christian faith for safety's sake and being out of danger he returned to the faith of his fathers, to which he had ever been faithful in his heart. He assumed the name of Jozef Nassi and then seemed to have two passions in life, a boundless ambition and a hatred of Christians. He succeeded in satisfying both, for he became a Bey and later on Duke of Naxos and the Cycladian Isles and avenged the persecution he had experienced. As already said the figure of this Portuguese-Turkish Jew was known and feared in Christian Europe and if not otherwise, Marlowe certainly knew his story from hearsay.

Now there is some similarity between the false notions Marlowe must have entertained about Machiavellianism and the false notions that were current about the Jews. The literature of his own country and its tradition confirmed him in his opinion. Then he knew a story about a mighty Jew, a Governor of Naxos and the Cycladian Isles, whose hatred of Christians is familiar to all Christian Europe. He was a playwright and eager for new subject matter. He knew what would please the public. He knew the figure of the Jew had always been a success and of course the idea occurred to him to fuse what he knew about Machiavelli, Jozef Nassi and Jews in general and work it into a drama,

and thus he gave the 'Jew of Malta' to the world. As
this drama shows the odd way in which the Jew in
literature is dealt with, in nearly all phases, I shall give
a survey of it and as I go along, comment on it.

In the prologue spoken at court, Marlowe says already, "we pursue the story of a *rich* and *famous* Jew
who lived in *Malta*: you shall find him still, in all his
projects, a sound Machiavill; and that's his character".
First of all it is the *rich* Jews of the Midde Ages, who
got such a firm hold of the imagination of the Christians, that even until this very day in spite of the obvious poverty of most of them, there are those who
cannot think of Jews without coupling them to money-
bags. The *famous* Jew may refer to Jožef Nassi and
Malta to one of the isles he was Governor of. The state
in which Malta found itself, however, resembled that
in which Florence was at the time of Machiavelli, as I
shall show later on. As for his Machiavellian character
and projects, I refer to what I said about Machiavelli
and the passions of ambition and revenge which dominated both him and Joan Miquez. We clearly see that
Marlowe intends to dramatise Machiavelli's philosophy,
but instead of taking the Italian Christian Statesman or
a Cæsar Borgia, he will take a Jew for reasons which
I have already mentioned.

A second prologue to the play is spoken by 'Machiavel'
himself, who in a few lines expounds his philosophy
and winds up by saying "I come to present the tragedy
of a Jew, who smiles to see how full his bags are
crammed; which money was not got without my means.
I crave but this.... let him not be entertained the
worse because he favours me," which removes all

obstacles against indentifying Machiavelli with the Jew.

In the first act Barabas is discovered in his counting house with heaps of gold before him. The actor no doubt will have looked like a genuine Jew in face,bearing and clothes and no doubt will have tried his level best to imitate his idiosyncrasies in gesture and speech with due exaggeration, as had been customary on the English stage.

The heaps of gold are a spectacular trick, as I do not suppose it was the custom of any tradesman to keep his gold displayed in such a way [1], but as mise-en-scène it was the very thing required.

Barabas is chiefly a Merchant, not a Usurer in the first place. and he indulges in a monologue conveying to the audience the fact that the Jew is a merchant-prince controlling the trade of the world, which is based on history. Equally historically true is the touch that, while exulting in his riches, the thoughts of peril and calamity do not leave him and therefore it is his ideal to inclose his infinite riches in a little room, so as to be able to carry them along in case. of attack or expulsion. There is nothing at first that is un-Jewish, on the contrary here and there touches occur that make Barabas a genuine Jew, thus for instance, when a merchant says, "they wondered how you durst with so much wealth trust such a crazed vessel, and so far", Barabas' answer "Tush, they are wise! I know her and her strength. But go, go thou thy ways, discharge thy ship and bid my factor bring his loading in", is a Jew's way of speaking. After some interruptions

[1] In fact on page 207 Ithamore says, that Barabas hides and buries his treasure under the earth. (Everyman's Library).

Barabas continues his monologue and shows an odd
mixture of Jew, Machiavellian and Mammon-worshipper.
The greatest gift that Heaven can bestow is wealth
and this he considers the blessings promised to the
Jews, and therein was old Abraham's happiness.

The spiritual blessings of the Jews he seems to have
swapped for Machiavellianism, for he laughs at conscience and rails at the Christian faith, the fruits of
which seem to be malice, falsehood, and excessive pride.
Except the touch of Machiavellianism there is not yet
anything improbable in the Jew's character, certainly
not when he declares that he has but one sole daughter,
whom he holds as dear as can be and for whom he
accumulates all his wealth. In my opinion this part
shows that Marlowe had some knowledge of Jews,
but now he leaves reality behind and soars into
wild, fanciful Machiavellianism, but for a genuine
Jewish touch here and there.

A Turkish fleet has come to Malta to claim the tribute
money the Maltese have neglected to pay for ten years.
This distress of Malta reflects, perhaps, the distress of
Florence, which had to endure degradation and extortion, to submit to the mandates of foreign powers, to
buy over and over again, at an enormous price, what
was already justly her own. The Turkish embassy is
entertained, a meeting is held in the senate-house and
the Jews are summoned to appear. They suspect danger
and in their fear flock to Barabas, who, instead of
acting as the Jews in history did and standing by his
brethren, behaves like a smooth ambiguous Italian
statesman, only having an eye to the main chance. He
guesses the true meaning of the arrival of the Turkish

fleet, knows that the Jews will be plundered and instead of advising the other Jews to bring as much of their wealth into safety as they can, says nothing but empty words and hides a great part of his own property. Here is the danger that he had always suspected and now he has much wealth that he can store in a little room. Things turn out as he has surmised. The Jews have to pay the tribute that has fallen due. As of old the Jews had to procure the money, half their fortune they must pay or turn Christians; if they refuse, they shall absolutely lose all they have. The Jews submit. Barabas having hidden part of his treasure plays the hero, refuses to pay half, refuses to become a Christian and must yield all he has. He scolds his brethern for their cowardice. Of course he acts this Machiavellian comedy to avert suspicion. That the Governor does not scruple thus to rob the Jews, is explained by the words which a knight speaks to Barabas, when the latter protests. He (the knight) says, "If your first curse fall heavy on thy head and make thee poor and scorned of all the world, 't is not our fault, but thy inherent sin", an opinion generally held at that time and which I shall refer to later on. So Barabas is robbed of all and his house or mansion converted into a nunnery.

In passing I should like to mention a few things that show Marlowe's ignorance regarding Jewish customs. To make a Jew speak of Agamemnon and Iphigen, when he wants an example of paternal love is bad, to make him kneel is worse, but to make him swear *Corpo* di Dio! is worst of all[1].

---

[1] To errors of this kind based upon ignorance must be added the fact that Jews are often mixed up with Mahometans. Gerontus, for instance, swears by Mahomet.

Here it is for the last time that we hear something of the other Jews, who disappear from the scene, as if the earth had swallowed them. Yet Marlowe is kind enough not to let them go without crediting them with some compassion for Barabas, whom they think utterly ruined. All the blacker is Barabas, who persists in his Machiavellian rôle and will not be consoled, and laughs at them, when they have turned their backs.

Here enters Abigail. She is fourteen years old and a beauty, as for her character it is sufficient for the present to say that she is an innocent lamb and if she does things that innocent lambs do not do as a rule, it is only because she is prompted by filial love and obedience to the will of her father, in whom she has the most perfect confidence, until his true character is revealed to her. In order to get back his treasure, which he has hidden in his house, which had been turned into a nunnery, Abigail becomes a novice there, not without remonstrating, but he teaches her in a true Machiavellian way, saying among other things "religion hides many mischiefs from suspicion". Barabas succeeds in obtaining his treasure and half mad with joy, hugs his bags. Now he is rich once more, his daughter is at home in his new house, a great and fair one as is the governor's, and revenge becomes his sole purpose in life.

Abigail, just like Jessica in *The Merchant of Venice*, is loved by a Christian, Mathias, the only son of a widow. Lodowick, the sun of the Governor, likewise falls in love with fair Abigail. In a true Machiavellian way Barabas incites the rivals, so that they kill each other. In effecting his villanies he makes use of a Turkish slave, Ithamore, and thus Marlowe involves the equally hated Turk in the Jew's crimes. Like master like man. When the Jew instructs Ithamore, the Machiavellian monster is revealed in all its horror. Macaulay speaking about the writings of Machiavelli says "It is indeed scarcely possible for any person, not well acquainted with the history and literature of Italy, to read without horror and amazement the celebrated treatise which has brought so much obloquy on the name of Machiavelli. Such a display of wickedness, naked yet not ashamed, such cool, judicious, scientific atrocity, seemed rather to belong to a fiend than to the most depraved of men. Principles which the most hardened ruffian would scarcely hint to his most trusted accomplice, or avow, without the disguise of some palliating sophism, even to his own mind, are professed without the slightest circumlocution, and assumed as the fundamental axioms of all political science." Now simply change the last words, 'axioms of all political science', into 'axioms of the art of living' and you have Marlowe's Jew. In illustration of the above I shall quote one of Barabas' speeches addressed to Ithamore.

> Hast thou no trade? then listen to my words,
> And I will teach (thee) that shall stick by thee:
>> First, be thou void of these affections,
>> Compassion, love, vain hope, and heartless fear;
>> Be mov'd at nothing, see thou pity none,
>> But to thyself smile when the Christians moan.
> As for myself, I walk abroad o' nights,
> And kill sick people groaning under walls:
> Sometimes I go about and *poison wells*;
> And now and then, to cherish Christian thieves,

I am content to lose some of my crowns,
That I may, walking in my gallery,
See 'em go pinion'd along by my door.
Being young I *studied physic* and began
To practise first upon the Italian;
There I enriched the priests with burials,
And always kept the sexton's arms in ure
With digging graves and ringing dead men's knells:
And, after that, was I an engineer,
And in the wars 'twixt France and Germany,
Under pretence of helping Charles the Fifth,
Slew friend and enemy with my stratagems:
Then, after that, I was an *usurer*,
And with extorting, cozening, forfeiting,
And tricks belonging unto brokery,
I fill'd the gaols with bankrupts in a year,
And with young orphans planted hospitals;
And every moon made some or other mad.
And now and then one hang himself for grief,
Pinning upon his breast a long great scroll
How I with interest tormented him.
But mark how I am blest for plaguing them;
I have as much coin as will buy the town.

When Abigail has learned the truth about her lover's death, she complains, "I perceive there is no love on earth, pity in Jews, nor piety in Turks" and becomes a nun in good earnest. Upon hearing this Barabas not only curses her bitterly, but decides to cause her death, which he does by poisoning the whole nunnery. Before dying, however, she confesses her father's crime to a friar, Barnardine, which confession leads up to another crime, for no sooner has Barabas perceived that this friar is acquainted with his crime, than he sets about to destroy him in the same way as he did his daughter's lover. He pretends that he wants to become a Christian and give his wealth to the monastery. Another friar, Jacomo, who is present when he speaks about his intention, tries to persuade him to come to his monastery. Barabas invites Barnardine to his house and strangles him there assisted by Ithamore. They take the body, set it upright against the wall, and put a staff into its hand. Jacomo coming there, thinks Barnardine stands there to prevent him from going to Barabas and strikes at him, the result being that he is thought to be his murderer and is hanged for killing him.

A thief and a whore living in Malta are trying to rob Barabas, but soon discover a far safer way to obtain his wealth. The whore Bellamira attracts Ithamore and soon they discover that Ithamore knows things about Barabas, which could send him to the gallows, and now they begin to milk the Jew. Barabas soon discovers how the land lies and by a trick poisons the thief, the whore and his servant. The poison does not work quickly and before his victims die, they reveal his crimes. When officers come to punish the Jew, they find him dead. This, however, is only a new trick and when his body is thrown over the walls to be a prey for vultures and wild beasts, he rises and says "I 'll be revenged on this accursed town; for by my means Calymath (who lays siege to Malta as they did not pay tribute) shall enter in .... I hope to see the governor a slave". All this is accomplished and Barabas is made governor of the town. But the town hates the Jew and he hits upon the following Machiavellian trick, which he communicates to Ferneze, so that the latter may see in him a friend and liberator of Malta. He invites the whole Turkish army and will banquet them in a monastery, under which there are explosives enough to kill all. As for Calymath and his consorts, for

him he has made a dainty gallery, the floor whereof, a
cable being cut, will fall asunder so that it sinks into
a deep pit past recovery. Ferneze pretends to agree
and the army is killed, but he manages to save Calymath
and make Barabas sink into the pit in a cauldron, where
he is burned to death, but not before cursing all soundly.

According to Macaulay, Machiavelli was wicked indeed,
but by the side of his wickedness he had many brilliant
qualities and even virtues. Barabas, however, has not
a single redeeming point in his character. The drama is
merely a very catalogue of crimes and sins; manners,
morals and laws are trodden down, and why? Only
because Barabas is seemingly, not really, thwarted in
his career as an accumulator of wealth. This Jew
retaliates upon society like a veritable devil, killing
right and left, till he is caught at last like a rat in the
trap he had set for his enemies.

Shylock. — *The Merchant of Venice* was written
between 1583 and 1593[1] and its popularity was remarkable[2]. It brings us to the most famous Jew of English
literature to Shakespeare's Shylock. I shall summarize
the contents of *The Merchant of Venice* as far as the
Jew is concerned. This tragi-comedy is the crowning
glory of the literary products dealing with the Jew.

Antonio loves his kinsman Bassanio with an almost
unnatural love and to oblige him, tries to borrow

[1] Grætz in *Shylock in den Sagen, etc.*, gives 1594 as the date of its appearance
(p. 29).

[2] "In 1701 Geo. Granville produced a comedy called "The Jew of Venice",
altered from Shakepeare's "Merchant"; but the alterations rather lessen than
improve the beauty and effect of the matchless original. The character of
Shylock, as Rowe remarks, is made comic, and we are prompted to laughter,
instead of detestation. In the second act a musical masque was introduced,
called Peleus & Thetis."

a sum of money from the Jew Shylock. Antonio hates Shylock with the profound Christian hatred so unreservedly demonstrated in English literature, besides this they are competitors and Antonio often hinders Shylock's trade, especially as a moneylender. Antonio openly gives vent to his unchristian hatred, spitting and kicking the Jew in the Rialto. This paragon of virtue comes and insolently asks for the loan of 3000 ducats. Here was a chance of revenge. Antonio's capital was locked up in ships. Ships are but boards, sailors but men, then there are pirates, storms and rocks. Of course the chances were a hundred to one that Antonio would be able to pay back the money with interest, but there was nevertheless a small chance that he would not. The Jew was ready to forego his sure profits in hopes of gratifying his ancient grudge and being revenged on his tormentor. Ostensibly to be friends with him and gain his good will or to buy his favour, he offers to lend the money gratis, and by way of joke he stipulates that a pound of flesh, to be cut from whatever part of the debtor's body he likes, will be forfeited in case the debtor should be in default. Antonio puts his seal unto this bond and calls Shylock a gentle Jew.

Meanwhile Shylock's daughter, his only child, elopes with a Christian, after robbing her father of a considerable amount of gold and jewels, which increases his desire for revenge and when Antonio is in default, he insists without pity on his pound of flesh. This is granted to him, but not a drop of blood shall be spilled and thus the Jew is defeated, and because, as an alien, he has sought the life of a citizen, one half of his goods may be seized by his victim and the other half by the state, while his life is at the Duke's mercy.

He is not killed and the greater part of his wealth is restored to him upon the condition that he turns Christian, and upon his death will leave all his property to his daughter and her husband, which conditions he accepts. The following extract [1] from Friedlander's Shakespeare and the Jew will account for its remarkable popularity. "Why did Shakespeare (or Marlowe) trouble to write a play about a Jew? Dit he know any Jews? He certainly knew them from the pages of history, from tales, legends, novels and poetry (and from the religious drama). There is very good reason to suppose that he (and also Marlowe) actually knew at least one in the flesh (and many more as Lee has shown). I am alluding to Dr. Lopez, the converted Jewish physician of Queen Elizabeth. Shakespeare must have been deeply interested in this man, who came from Portugal to England in 1559. His ability as a member of the medical profession was duly recognised by his English colleagues. Not only was he appointed royal physician, but he was also employed by the government by reason of his extensive foreign correspondence (think of Barabas' extensive relations). In 1592 the Earl of Essex welcomed to England a Portuguese adventurer, Don Antonio, who was a pretender to the Spanish throne, and Lopez acted as the fugitive's interpreter. Lopez and Antonio did not remain friends for long. Moreover, Essex suspected that Lopez was in the pay of Elizabeth's enemy, Philip, King of Spain, and was conspiring to poison Queen Elizabeth and Don Antonio. When the matter

[1] The enclosures in this quotation are my own. H. M.

was brought to the Queen's attention she expressed incredulity, but Essex undertook to prove the accusation true and he left no stone unturned to bring together sufficient evidence to secure a conviction. The Queen signed the death-warrant with reluctance. After the execution of Lopez, Queen Elizabeth granted certain property to the widow and children of the unfortunate Jew. Was it probable that the Queen would give such a gift to the widow of a man who actually attempted to poison her? This was all the Queen could do by way of reparation, knowing that her late physician was innocent. Shakespeare knew Marlowe's Jew of Malta, Barabas. He, like Dr. Lopez, is a physician. Barabas admits having poisoned wells and killed people. Directly after the execution of Lopez the Jew of Malta was staged repeatedly, and in the same year *The Merchant of Venice* was performed for the first time. This event took place on August 23rd 1594, only a few months after the public execution of the converted Jew." From a number of places and allusions, for which see Friedlander pp. 19 ff. and Lee in the Gentleman's Magazine (Febr., 1880, pp. 183 ff.) we may pretty surely conclude that Shakespeare had Lopez in his mind, when he was writing the Merchant of Venice.

Massinger's Duke of Milan. — Both Machiavelli and the Jewish doctor acting as a poisoner are reflected in. three other plays written by lesser stars. In *The Duke of Milan*, written by Massinger, one of the characters, Francisco the special favourite of Sforza, besmears the lips of the dead heroine, the Duke's wife, with poison, so that the Duke dies in kissing her. Francisco does so, disguised as a Jewish doctor.

"Machiavellus". — Judging from this we need not expect an exemplar of probity in the Jew who occurs in the following play ascribed to Massinger. Douce, the Shakesperian scholar, mentions a play acted at Cambridge in 1597 called *Machiavellus*, in which the bearer of the title rôle and the real hero of the play, a Jew, Jacuppes, carry on a contest, with a remarkable series of disguises, plots and counter plots, for the hand of the heroine, Orlanda, with whom Jacuppes is madly in love. He puts poison in her wine which acts as a sleeping draught and intends to dig her up, when she is once buried, to restore her to life and marry her. This contest between Jacuppes and Machiavellus goes on till the heroine's betrothed, who is supposed to have been killed in the wars, returns just in time to claim her once more as his own. A copy of this play is in the Bodleian Library (MS. Douce 234) [1]. So we see once more that as a matter of fact the Jew and the Christian Machiavelli are considered as members of the same brotherhood.

Greene's Selimus. — Quite in keeping with the opinion in vogue at that time about the Jew is an anonymous play, describing the career of an Eastern barbaric potentate, entitled *Selimus*. The play is ascribed to Robert Greene, together with whose works it is printed in Dr. Grosart's edition. Selimus wars against his own father Bajazet, whom he causes to be poisoned by the Jew, as I shall mention below, and murders his two brothers. The Jew Abraham is taken up in the train

[1] S. Lee, *Elizabethan England and the Jews*.

of Bajazet. He is a cunning fellow, professing physic and so skilled in it, that it seems as if he has power over life and death; withal a man so stout and resolute that he will venture anything for gold. He will poison Selimus father with some intoxicating drink, which he offers Bajazet (and his wife) as a remedy. But Bajazet orders him to drink first and the Jew quickly deliberating that he is an old man already and will not live much longer, drinks of the cup of poison and Bajazet and his wife Aga follow his example.

The Wisdom of Doctor Dodypoll. — About 1600 *The Wisdom of Doctor Dodypoll* appeared, a badly contrived patchwork, which in many respects reminds us of the Jew. In the first place the broken English spoken by the Doctor. In the second place his desire to marry the heroine (think of Jacuppus in *Machiavellus*). In the third place several traits which were at any rate thought to be Jewish. He has a servant called Zaccharee, which is a Jewish name. All this of course is not conclusive proof that a Jew was meant, but if no Jew was meant, most of the details were at any rate derived from the Jew of Literature.

Iacke Drum's Entertainment. — A similar play in which a figure appears equipped with all the fashionable Jewish peculiarities as seen at that time, without the name of Jew attached to it, is *Iacke Drum's Entertainment,* which was first published in 1601 and attributed to Marston. One of its prominent characters, is described in the dramatis personae as "Mammon the Usurer with a great firie nose". Of him it is said in the play, 'Oh Sir, Mamon is in a citie of Iurye (= Jewry) called Bethlem." He too woos the heroine of the play. He too is compared

with the devil. He is gouty, a peculiarity characteristic
of Jews, as I will show later on. He too has a servant who
pesters him. He too raves. In fact Creizenach, speaking
of this play in his *Geschichte des Neueren Drama*,
Vol. V, p. 225 says "Ihr (Catherines) zurückgewiesener
Liebhaber, der Wucherer Mammon, eine groteske
Figur, die in mancher Hinsicht an *Shylock* erinnert,
rächt sich, indem er Catherines Gesicht mit *Krotengift*
beschmiert und dadurch furchtbar entstellt, eine wider-
wärtige situation, die aus Sidneys *Arcadia* entlehnt ist."

The Travailes of the Three English Brothers. — In 1607
John Day and his coadjutors W. Rowley and G.
Wilkins composed a play based on history and named
The Travailes of the Three English Brothers. The historical facts are greatly exaggerated and as for the Jew
who occurs in it, we learn (from Nixon) that Sir Thomas
Sherley, when imprisoned at Constantinople, was
befriended by a kindhearted Jewish merchant. No doubt
it would have been a hazardous experiment to bring
on the stage a charitable Jew, but it is really too bad
that we should be afflicted, in the person of Zariph,
with a travesty of Shylock.

Sir Anthony Sherley and his brother Maister Robert
go to Persia, where they find favour with the Sophey,
who shows his manner of warfare, upon which Anthony
demonstrates his. Sir Anthony's guns are greatly ad-
mired. He is appointed General against the Turks,
persuades the Sophey to league with Christendom and
crave their aid against the Turk. To this the Sophey
agrees and Anthony is appointed ambassador. He is
accompanied by Hallibeck, a Persian gentlemen. This
Hallibeck loves the Sophey's niece, but the latter

prefers Anthony. Prompted by jealousy Hallibeck thwarts Anthony first at the Russian court and then at Rome. In the meantime the third brother Thomas after many adversities has been taken prisoner by the Turks and sends a message to his victorious brother Robert. In Rome Sir Anthony has dealings with Zariph, a Jew from Venice. He has bought a jewel for the Sophey and the money is due to Zariph, but he is not in a position to meet his engagement, as appears from the following extracts, showing close affinity to the *Merchant of Venice*.

Sir Anthony: Good morrow, honest Zariph.

Zariph: The Hebrew God and sanctified King bless them that cast kind greeting at the Jew.

Sir A.: I owe thee money.

Zariph: Thats the cause of your kind speech: A Christian spaniell clawes and fauns for gaine.

Iest on, deride the Jew. You may, vext Zariph will not iest with you. No by my soule, 't would my spirit much refresh to taste a banket all of Christian flesh.

Sir A.: I must intreat thee of forbearance.

Zariph: No, not an hour.

Here Zariph turns to a 'Gentleman' saying: "You sold my brother Zacharie like a horse, his wife and children at a common outcrie." To this the 'Gentleman' replies: "That was the Law",

Zariph: I desire no more: tho the Iew be poore he shall have law for money.

Sir A.: Strangers to strangers should be pitifull.

Zariph: If we be curst we learn't of Christians, who like swine crash one anothers bones.

"But they are Christians; Zariph is a Jew, a crucifying Hang-man trayn'd in sinne, one that would hang his brother for his skinne". Zariph says, he will bear with him a day to show that Jews are better than Christians for "Theile not forbeare a minute." Sir Anthony invites him for a banquet. Zariph replies "No bankets, yet I thank you with my heart, — (aside) and vow to play Iew; why tis my part." At that feast the Jew has Anthony arrested. Venting his spleen and the grudge he bears, he gives utterance to his pent up feelings of hatred towards the Christians, for this, that and the other thing, in a current of abuse; he raves like a madman [1], grinning, laughing, mad with you at his revenge.

However, things turn out favourable for the three brothers. The Jew's affair is only an incident in their adventures; Zariph is introduced as an instrument to bring about the unmerited temporary ruin of one of them and apparently to gratify the audience, who must have thought the Jew-scene thrilling and diverting.

Robert Daborne's A Christian turned Turk. — In 1612 a new play appeared *A Christian turned Turk* by Robert Daborne. It is a story of Violence, Lucre and Lust. Captain Ward, a freebooter, sights a pursued vessel and captures it. The captain of the pursuing ship wants to share the booty, which Ward refuses to do. A duel ensues. While the two captains are fighting, one of Ward's men, Gallop, sails away with the prize, which he intends to keep for himself.

A third captain is now introduced, Dansiker, who has been pardoned by the King of France and now

---

[1] This raving seems to be an inheritance from Herod. Benwash, Shylock, Barabas, all rave like madmen, which seems to be part of the character.

wants to make amends for his past robberies by ruining all the pirates that lie in the harbour of Tunis, which seems to be a gathering-place for the free gentlemen of the sea, the freebooters and pirates. To this town Gallop comes with his twice stolen ship, and later on also Ward and the captain of the pursuing vessel, Francisco, with whom Ward had contracted friendship.

In a place where so many thieves come together we expect a Jew, of course, and indeed there lives one, who is an apostate into the bargain, for he has become a Turk. He is a usurer, a cruel slavedealer, a bawd, a receiver of stolen goods. He has a wife and a sister-in-law. These are no Jewesses, but Turkish women. The Jew's name is Benwash. He prostitutes his sister-in-law and his wife makes him a cuckold.

So all captains and Gallop have put into the harbour of Tunis, where lucre brings them into contact with Benwash, and lust with his wife and her sister. Benwash is deceived by his wife with Gallop, therefore he makes his servant Rabshake strangle his wife and murder Gallop. The servant is killed in his turn by his wily master, who by a clever trick passes the men of the sea and Dansiker as the murderers. Francisco and Dansiker are hanged by the hangman. The Jew, however, dies as well, saying, "Bear witnesse though I lived a Turke, I dye a Iew". As the fates of the others are not immediately connected with the Jew, they need not be detailed here.

Decker's Jew of Venice. — The English actors who towards the end of the 16th and in the early part of the 17th century were in the habit of making professional tours in Germany and Austria, included in their reper-

tory a confusing play apparently constructed out of
Marlowe's Jew and Shakespeare's Merchant (Cf. Meissner, *Die Englische Comoedianten zur Zeit Shakespeares
in Oesterreich*, 1884, pp. 130—189, where the play is
printed from a Viennese MS.). This play is indentified
by some with Decker's *Jew of Venice* in which a Jew
is said to have played the principal part and which is
dated about 1605. Before the Jew enters, Decker, if he
be the author, starts with the prosecution of the Jews
in, and their banishment from Cyprus, thus giving some
reason for his Jew's subsequent behaviour. As this
play is either based on Shakespeare and Marlowe, or
founded upon their sources, it is not necessary to deal
with it separately.

Newes from Hell. — In *Newes from Hell*, Decker reflects a Jewish usurer; he endows his hero with traits
of character that leave no room for doubt on this point.
At first, however, he does not mention the name of
Jew, he leaves us in the dark, perhaps to strain our
attention; subsequently, however, he calls this wretched
usurer, who, even in Hell, cannot abandon his way
of life, the rich Jew of Malta.

Beaumont and Fletcher's Custom of the Country. — In
The Custom of the Country (1619 or 1622) by Beaumont
and Fletcher we also come across a Jew. In this play
Arnoldo, a gentleman contracted to Zenocia, feels
miserable, and he has good reason to. The wicked custom
of the country (Italy) demands namely that the Governor
must have the maidenhead of every girl that is going
to be married or allow it to be ransomed by money.
In this case the Governor prefers the maidenhead.
Zenocia feels as miserable as her lover and on the same

ground of course. They marry and fly the country by means of a bark, but are pursued by the Governor.

Notwithstanding the pursuing vessel, their bark is taken by a third ship that puts in her appearance and the master of which is a sea-captain who is enamoured of one Hippolyta, a rich lady, who, however, in her turn is wantonly in love with Arnoldo. The bark is captured, the sea- captain claims Zenocia and Arnoldo jumps overboard. His example is followed by his bro- ther Rutilio, a merry gentleman. Leopold (this is the name of the enamoured sea-captain) is going to make a present of Zenocia to Hippolyta. Arnoldo and Ru- tilio are washed ashore and in their sad plight are met by the Jew Zabulon, servant to Hippolyta. Rutilio dares not hope the Jew will help him in his need, as courtesies come sooner from the Devil than from any of the Jew's nation. Zabulon, however, declares "We are men, and have like you, compassion, when we find fit subjects for our bounty". In spite of this humane trait our Jew is a pander, who knows how to arrange a luxurious banquet to lull asleep Arnoldo's scruples as regards Hippolyta's intentions; his efforts, however, are in vain. Hippolyta and Arnoldo's case is that of Venus and Adonis once more. As for our Jew there is nothing Jewish about him except his name and in this play, in which Chastity conquers Lust and purifies the impure, while all ends well, the Jew is only Lust's instrument to obtain its end by means of a *magic potion* and if this should be impossible, then he will have to avenge its thwarted desire, for the Jew will also procure a murderer, if needs be. In this play all turn good in the end and even the Jew is supplied with means that he may afford the luxury of living according to the law. The Jew and all that is evil are introduced only and solely to show the power of purity.

Webster's The Devil's Law-case. — In Webster's *The Devil's Law-case* (Act V) one personage dresses again like a Jewish doctor, namely Romeo. He appears in the habit of a Jew, a rare Italianated Jew. The qualities of a Jew are enumerated and it is, as if Webster racks his brain and ransacks history and literature, but especially the latter, to find as many vices and crimes as he possibly can to blacken the Jew. Here is the Machiavellian again with his several changes of faces. Here is the hypocrite who winds about a man like rotten ivy and eats into him like quicksilver, the poisoner of a friend, the giver of a drench which makes a man linger of nine years while the rascal makes it seem a natural disease, the coiner of money, the corrupter of ladies' honours. Betraying a town to the Turk or making a bonfire of the Christian navy is just what suits this traitor, who swears upon his Jewism.

Thomas Goffe's The Raging Turk. — Nearly forty years after its first appearance the story of Selimus was again treated in another tragedy, where Abraham the Jew, under the new name of Hamon, plays his old part, namely in *The Raging Turk, or Bajazet II*, by Thomas Goffe in 1631. This Hamon is no pure fiction. Nicholas de Nicholay [1] mentions a Hebrew, Amon, as having the first dignity and authority amongst the order of 'phisition', a person much esteemed for his goods, knowledge and renown as for honour and port-

---

[1] Nicholas Nicholay *Navigations*, translated by F. Washington the younger. London, 1585.

liness. That such a character should be degraded into a foul murderer is again an example of the liberty the dramatists were used to allow themselves as regards history, when the Jews were concerned.

John Ford's Perkin Warbeck. — In John Ford's *Perkin Warbeck*, Act 5 Scene 3, we come across the following statement as to Warbeck's father. "Your father was a Jew turned Christian to repair his miseries". In this Ford follows Speed's History where we find that this youth (Perkin) was born, they say in the city of Torney and called Peter Warbeck, the son of a converted Jew, whose godfather at baptism King Edward IV himself was. Bernard André, the court chronicler to Henry VII says that they pretended that a certain Peter, a native of Tournai, who had been brought up thereabouts by one Edward, once a Jew, but afterwards laved in the sacred font by King Edward, was the younger son of Edward IV.

Cecil Roth in *The Jewish Historical Society*, Vol. IX, traces this Jew to one Sir Edward Brampton who lived about 1468, alias Edward Brandon, and tells us the wonderfully adventurous life of this converted Jew [1].

Richard Brome, The Jewish Gentleman. — We started with *The Three Ladies of London* the only play extant in which a Jew was fairly treated and we might have ended with a similar one. But unfortunately the play has got lost. About 1640 Richard Brome is said to have written a play entitled *The Jewish Gentleman,* and in *Elizabethan England and the Jew*, S. Lee says, it is a pity that this play should have got lost, for in it,

[1] See page 38.

as in *The Three Ladies of London*, the Jew seems to have been treated in a favourable manner.

Peele's The Love of King David and Fair Bethsabe. — I have not included *The Love of King David and Fair Bethsabe* by Peele (1599) in the plays dealt with, for the simple reason that this is based on the Old Testament and nothing specially Jewish occurs in it. Moreover the author would not have introduced anything disagreeable for reasons which I have already explained at the outset.

Hemings' The Jewes Tragedy. — Strange to say, however, there is a play *The Jewes Tragedy* (1662) by William Hemings, a younger contemporary of Shakespeare, in which the Jews might have been depicted with the black colours usually employed for this malicious race, but they are not. It lacks all confessional elements, and contains no points of traditionally or really Jewish peculiarity. It deals with the downfall of the Jewish Kingdom and the conquest and devastation of Jeruzalem. With the exception of this play, *The Three Ladies* and perhaps *The Jewish Gentleman* (if we leave out the Jew of the Gospel) we may say that it is in his exile, when the Jew is poaching on Christian preserves that Christian authors look upon him as an intruder, a rival, a nuisance and that their malice is roused accordingly.

The Name of 'Jew'. — 'What is in a name?' Shakespeare asks. There need be nothing, there may be and often there is a good deal in it! Let us trace the name of 'Jew' and see what is in it.

In Anglo-Saxon the name Jew is either used to denote one of the ancient people without any additional meaning, or one of those who behaved in some unkind or cruel manner in connection with the Saviour. This second use of the word created a prejudice against all bearers of the name. In this second stage the word occurs as early as 1225 (Murray [1]). But then it had already far advanced into the third phase of its development on account of the Jews' stay in England, and from something vague, phantomlike, it had come to denote a creature with more shape, colour and spirit. "Ich holde me vilore then a Gyw" (Murray [1]) leaves no doubt about the meaning of the name. Finally, at the end of the 17th century, it has reached the summit and stands for a tangible monster, the grasping, extortionate moneylender, the driver of hard bargains, the crafty dealer. The expression 'bloudie or bloody Jew' occurs in *The Travels of the Three Brothers* and refers to his crucifying, poisoning and otherwise murdering, innocent Christians. The instances of the word Jew used in its worst sense, are so numerous [1] that it would be quite superfluous to mention some examples. The expression 'bloody Jew' is still in force nowadays among the lower classes. Ferneze, the Governor of Malta, wanting to obtain their money, addresses them with the word Hebrews, which seems to have been a politer way of calling them, and which, therefore, is hardly ever used.

Bearing and Physiognomy. — Let us now build up the creature labelled 'Jew', deriving our materials from the literary works mentioned before and start by fixing his bearing and facial expression.

---

[1] A great many instances are given by Lee and in Murray's New English Dictionary under "Jew".

The world judges from appearances, for the very good reason that in most cases it has very little else to judge from and is too lazy or unable to look below the surface. Therefore the outward appearance given to a character in Art is of sovereign importance, for this ultimately creates what is called 'general opinion'. That the inward appearance bestowed upon a character in Art is of equal importance is a matter of course and need not be emphasized. "Art takes life as part of her rough material, recreates it, and refashions it in fresh forms, is absolutely indifferent to fact". "A great artist invents a type, and Life tries to copy it, to reproduce it in a popular form, like an enterprising publisher." I am not sure, whether these quotations from Oscar Wilde hold good in every respect, but in the case of the Jew in early English literature, they contain nothing but truth. Thus early English literary art took the living Hebrew as a part of her rough material, recreated him, and refashioned him in a fresh form, and was absolutely indifferent to fact. The then artists invented a type, 'the Jew', and society equally indifferent to fact copied, took over this Jew, was blind to every other possibility, considered it as something absurd that a Jew might be something unlike *that* Jew. That is to say, little by little the English people were taught to see the Jew in a queer grotesque way, so much so, that at last they could not see him in any other way. Their teachers, the clergy and the dramatists picked out all the peculiar outward features and the inward traits of character that could be made ridiculous or odious and built up a type that rouses our laughter and disgust in turns.

Matthew Paris explicitly states that the Jewish usurer was *courteous* in business towards his debtor. Francis Bacon [1], who was never well disposed towards the Jew Lopez, whom we may consider to be the original of Shylock, wrote of him as "a man very *observant* and *officious*, and of a *pleasing* and *pliable* behaviour", which I call a concise but fair description of an average Jew, and a friend of Leicester speaks of Lopez as a very *honest* and *zealous* person. So, courteous, observant, officious, pleasing, pliable, honest and zealous. A number of qualities which I think are strictly necessary for the Jew, if he wants to live and thrive among his enemies, qualities, which circumstances and their position would have naturally developed in them, if they had not already possessed them. These qualities may easily degenerate into servility, cringing, fawning, hypocrisy and bigotry, and no doubt there may have been Jews guilty of them, why not? But it is obviously malicious to make *the* Jew, the respresentative of his race, possessed of these vices. I am inclined to believe that the Jews of the Middle Ages were more timid than bold, though over and over again they have given proofs of the greatest moral and physical courage; but to see their timidity habitually stigmatized as cowardice strikes me as a misrepresentation. The Jew's physiognomy is more lively, more expressive of emotional states than that of the Christian, a smile sooner appears, so does an expression of impatience or of temper. Does this justify the authors, however, to represent him as either grinning or with a face contorted with passion? The Jew in the Middle Ages was sooner

[1] *A True Report of Dr. Lopez his Treason* by Francis Bacon, 1594.

ready to vent his spleen in an outburst of words than to come to blows, must he therefore be represented as noisy, raging, swearing and cursing? His mode of living and his sedentary life of a student of law excluded sport and games, but was this reason to represent him as practically deformed? No doubt his sense of superiority and sharpened wit will from time to time have induced him to make the Christian feel them both, but this certainly did not prove him to be either a haughty creature or a scoffer. Jews gesticulate more than Englishmen or Dutchmen, but it is silly to represent them as unable to control their movements.

The early English artists have been guilty of violating truth by representing the Jew in the odd way described above as I will show below by quoting passages from the literary productions mentioned by me.

Thus Marlowe makes Barabas say, "we Jews can *fawn* like *spaniels* when we please; and when we *grin* we bite; yet are our looks as innocent and harmless as a lamb's" (*The Jew of Malta*, Act II). We know that a fawning or cringing person is called a spaniel [1] and Marlowe may have wanted to draw attention to the country of origin of many Jews, to Spain, as well as to their outward appearance, for this sort of dog is generally described as having a long silky coat and drooping ears. In early literature the Jew is generally called a dog! Thus Shylock says, (Act. III, Sc. III). "Thou call'dst me dog before thou hadst a cause". These and suchlike expressions make us see the Jew like a stray dog, fearing and hating the Christian and yet in an abject way, always hoping to get something

[1] Murray, New English Dictionary.

out of him in true canine fashion. When conversing with a Christian, the Jew is represented as fawning and grovelling. A good example of this is given in *The Merchant of Venice*, Act. I, Sc. III lines 55, 56.

When Sir Anthony in the *Travels of the Three Brothers* asks for postponement of payment, the stage directions were no doubt that he should do so in a polite way, which enables the Jew to retaliate and taunt, "Thats the cause of your kind speech: a Christian spaniell clawes and fauns for gaine."

Quite in keeping with the above are the words of Barabas, (Act. II) "I learned in Florence how to kiss my hand, heave up my shoulders when they call me dog, and duck as low as any bare-foot friar."

As soon as the Jew feels safe, however, and has some power, then his attitude changes, then he becomes haughty and conceited, he laughs impudently or mockingly, scoffs derisively, gibes and sneers or boasts as the case requires. It is this attitude the Jew of Malta strikes (Act. IV) that makes Pilia-Borza say "then, like a Jew, he laughed and jeered". In the same way Ferneze says of Barabas "How the slave jeers at him!" As for bragging and boasting, the passages in *The Jew of Malta* are very numerous, while Herod, as he figures in the mysteries, is perhaps the prototype of the braggard on the stage. Another striking peculiarity is the Jew's gesticulation which has also come down from the Mysteries, especially his shrugging of shoulders. This has even come down to the present day and if a Jew must be represented on the stage, you may be sure he will shrug his shoulders. An instance of this we find in *The Merchant of Venice* (Act I. Sc. III. 97), where

Shylock says "Still have I born it with a patient shrug".

His body. — This leads us on to the body of the Jew.
A comparison between one race and another, will lead
every unprejudiced judge to the conclusion that both
races have fine and bad specimens and that it would
certainly be unfair to take the bad specimens and set
them up as representatives of the whole race. The Jews
certainly have not many snub-noses amongst them,
but to provide every Jew with the beak of an eagle is
equally absurd as to adorn every Englishman with the
snout of a bull-dog.

The most prominent feature of the Jew in literature
and on the stage that has always excited merriment is
that prominently prominent one, his nose. One of the
principal characters in *Iacke Drum's Entertainment*
(1601) is described in the dramatis personae as "Mammon the Usurer withe a great firie Nose" besides
being *gouty*. In *The Jew of Malta* Ithamore refers three
times to his master's nose. "I have the bravest bottle-
nosed knave to my master." This bottle-nose he has
in common with the Devil, whose "bottle-nose" and
"evil face" are mentioned in Ulpian Fulwell's Like
will to Like. "O, brave Master"!, Ithamore calls out,
"I worship your nose for this" and again "God-a-mercy
nose!" Of course the Jew's face is yellow-skinned, his
hair and beard [1] are black or have the Judas-colour
red. Red was also the colour of Cain's beard. The Jew's
hands are claw-like as are the devil's hands. In 'A
Christian turned Turk' the Jewish servant gives
further information about the Jew's beauty by declaring

---

[1] The actor Richard Barbayn, who first acted the part of Shylock, wore a beard
like Lopez and this became traditional. Barabas also has a beard.

"the Jew is troubled (for the most part) with *gowty* legges and fiery nose."

We possess a portrait or probably a caricature which may be considered as the earliest sketch of a mediæval Jew. It is to be found in an entry on the Forest Roll of Essex now at the Record Office. It represents 'Aaron', son of the Devil, '*fil diaboli*', a Jew who lived in Colchester about 1267.

It shows deep set, piercing, expressive eyes with long upperlids, beetling brows, hooked nose and thick protruding nether lip. Another caricature of Jews is to be found at the top of an Issue Roll of the Exchequer. The figure represents Isaac of Norwich with three faces (probably to show his wide dealings), of which the striking features are the silly noses [1]). As the first caricature might just as well have been drawn to-day, I infer that throughout those ages the actors will no doubt have tried to represent a similar caricature on the stage when acting the part of a Jew.

His Dress. — Now the picture is complete but for the Jewish garb. There cannot be the least doubt that the Jew was dressed differently from the Christians. Thus Rutilio in *The Custom of the Country* recognizes the Jew by his habit. The servant, announcing Romeo in *The Devil's Law-case* disguised as a Jew doctor, says, "he has a strange aspect; a Jew by birth."

The only difficulty is to make out what that dress really consisted of. The sailors, who enter Benwash's house, find Gallop's trousers and say "these are none of the Jewes trousers".

[2] Four pictures of Jews are also to be found on pp. 188 and 189 of *Symbols of the Passion*, ed. by R. Morris, E. E. T. S. No. 46.

From a note to Act I, Sc. III of *The Merchant of Venice* [1] I learn that "Shylock doubtless was introduced with an orange-tawny bonnet, the mark of a Jew, with which compare Bacon's *Essays*, edited by Reynolds, p. 287, *On Usury*, where Bacon says that usurers should have orange-tawny bonnets because they do Judaize. The Jews in Europe during the Middle Ages were usually compelled to wear a distinguishing dress. This was commonly of yellow, it was sometimes a yellow cap, sometimes a yellow badge on the breast. According to Vecellio, quoted by Mr. Knight in his "Introductory Notice" to this play, the Jews of Venice were distinguished from the other citizens only by wearing a yellow bonnet, while Saint Didier, in his *Histoire de Venice*, says they wore scarlet hats lined with black taffeta. Mr. Hunter (*New Illustrations of Shakespeare*, Vol. 1. p. 299) reconciles these discrepant statements by a reference to Coryat (*Crudities*, p. 231) who describes the dress of the Jews: 'those born in Italy wearing red hats, while Eastern or Levantine Jews wore yellow turbans' . . . . as for Shylock's dress on the stage, it was probably merely conventional." This last statement I cannot entirely agree with. Shylock must have worn some special Jewish dress, for he says (in Act 1 Sc. III. l. 100) "You call me misbeliever, cut-throat dog, and spit upon my *Jewish gaberdine*". The Concise Oxford Dictionary explains this word as a long upper garment, esp. of Jews" and in a note to line 100 [1] I read: "Florio, 1611, gives the Italian 'Gavardina'. It was a *long* smockfrock of coarse material". As a final touch we must add the badge Pope Innocent III

[1] Clark and Wright. Clarendon Press Series, pp. 89 and 91.

ordained the Jew to wear. As regards the distinguishing
marks the Jew had to wear, we know some further
details. The Lateran Council of 1215 accentuated the
isolation of the Jews by ordering them to wear a distinctive mark, which in England took the characteristic
form of a piece of cloth attached to the upper garment
in the shape of the two tablets of the law as seen in
the Synagogues to the present day. In Green's *Short
History*, Chap. IV, Sec. V., we read "they (the Jews)
were forbidden to move through the streets without the
two *white* tablets of *wool* on their breast which distinguished their race". As we shall see colour and material
were subject to changes, just as was the reason why the
Jews had to wear these marks, thus we read that "to
complete their *security*, (that none might do them hurt,
under pretence of not knowing them) the king (Henry
III in 1216), by proclamation, order'd that they should
by way of distinction, wear upon the forepart of their
garment, two broad strippes of white linen, or parch-
ment". In an ordinance of St. Louis (1269) we read that
the marks of distinction were obligatory to Jews of
both sexes. In England a like order was made in Edward
the First's reign: 'E k (i. e. ke, que) checun Geu þus
kil avra passee set anz, porte enseine en son soverain
garnement, cest assav^r en forme de deus tables joyntes
de feutre jaune, and that each Jew that is past seven
years of age shall wear a badge upon his upper garment
in the form of two tables of *yellow* or saffron taffety. It
was to be six fingers long and three fingers broad. "What
mystery there was in thus changing the colour of their
badges I can 't guess", says Toovey, "unless white was
considered as an emblem of too great purity and yellow

substituted to denote envy and malice". The caricature
we have spoken of, shows indeed the Jew as wearing
this badge. [1]

His Smell. — For completeness' sake I add the following quotation from Toovey, although I do not remember
that in literature I have come across the expressions of
stinking or dirty Jew, which, however, have been quite
common in the mouths of their detractors until this
very day. "The author of Roma Santa takes notice,
upon such an occasion (baptism), that whereas Jews
naturally stink, they constantly lose that ill savour after
baptism. But Misson (*Voyage into Italy*) accounts for this
miracle, by answering, that before such sort of people
intend to appear in public, they take care to wash
themselves well and that their ill smell before baptism,
which prejudiced men think natural, arises from
sordidness of their habits, occasioned by poverty".

His Language. Swearing and Cursing. — Of greater
importance and certainly reflected in literature is the
Jew's language or rather the way in which he speaks
the language of the country he lives in. The Jews
had no permanent place of abode, at any rate many
were moving from one country to another and consequently we may suppose that the languages many
of them spoke were not faultless, besides they had
no doubt some language of their own, which they
used when they moved in their own circle of friends
and relations, and if we add to this that they generally
lived separated from the Christians, especially in their
childhood, which did not promote the correctness of their

---

[1] The badge is mentioned figuratively by Shylock, when he says, "Sufferance
is the badge of all our tribe".

pronunciation, we may safely conclude that their way of speaking the language of their Christian neighbours induced the latter to ridicule it. We find many instances of this from very early times. Herod already is represented as unable to speak his language well, which is absurd of course, as he was no Jew of the Diaspora and lived in his own country, but the writers of the Mysteries availed themselves of this means to make the Jews despicable and ridiculous even though the latter lived before the Diaspora. The Jew's gibberish and use of foreign words now and then is not restricted to him, but must be looked upon as one of the comical resources of the time. That the Jews of the New Testament are represented as speaking gibberish is of course a sort of anachronism, but that Barabas, Shylock, Dodypoll and the others are thus brought upon the stage may be in keeping with history. Barabas uses a hardly intelligible jargon between Italian and Spanish such as possibly may have been spoken by a Jew of Malta.

A peculiarity of the Jew's speech is his love of swearing and cursing. This is perhaps also founded upon truth. The first traces are found in the New Testament [1]. In Rollins's collection of ballads [2], p. 218, the Jew's swearing in business is mentioned, and before dying Barabas exclaims, "tongue, curse thy fill". In fact nearly all Jews in literature are more or less addicted to these bad habits and their language, physiognony and attitude are all expressive of passion.

His Soul and Character. — Up till now we have consider-

[1] Matthew 26. 74, and also in the Old Testament, Genesis 3.14 and 4.11, Leviticus 24.11, Deuteronomy 27.15, Samuel II, 16.7.
[2] *A Pepysian Garland*, Cambridge 1922.

ed his outward appearance; let us next have a look at
the motive power hidden beneath this ungainly surface,
which actuates this creation, let us reveal the soul, the
Jew's soul. It is a moot point, whether an animal has a
soul, but even those who think it has one, do not go so
far as to put it on a par with a human soul. This inferior
soul was thought good enough for the Jew. They
represented him as possessed of a bloodthirsty animal
spirit that had assumed a human shape, the werwolf
of ancient heathen mythology.

"Thou almost makest me waver in my faith to hold
opinion with Pythagoras, that souls of animals infuse
themselves into the trunk of men: thy currish spirit
govern'd a *wolf*, who hanged for human slaughter,
even from the gallows did his fell soul fleet, and,
whilst thou lay'st in thy unhallowed dam, infused itself,
in thee." (*Merchant of Venice*, Act IV, Sc. 1. 130).

Chaucer already says "Our firste fo, the *Serpent* Sathanas, That hath in Jewes herte his waspes nest",
etc. (*Prioresses Tale* line 1748).

Speaking of Sathanas reminds me of the fact that
the Jew is also constantly compared with, or really
possessed of the Devil. I think I have clearly demonstrated this in treating *St. Mary Magdalen* where Infidelity, the Vice of the play, boasts of being a devil,
the son of *the* Devil and says of himself that he sticks so
much in the Jews' heart that they will not believe the
doctrine of Jesus.

The devil is the spirit of evil, he is the enemy of
Christ and hates him. The devil and the Jew are possessed of the hatred of Christ in an equal degree. This
hatred is reflected from the earliest literature down to

Shakespeare and when, in the latter part of the period I deal with, the Jew figures chiefly as a usurer, this hatred must be considered as prevailing in so vehement a degree that it overrules his craving for money, which is one of his ruling passions. It seems as if the Devil and the Vice of the older drama have disappeared only to reappear in the regular drama in the shape of the Jew to frighten and amuse the audience. Another successor of the Devil was Machiavelli, as already shown, and the Devil, the Jew and Machiavelli form the Unholy Trinity of early English literature embodied in the Jew. The Machiavellian character of the Jew appears from the following lines, quoted from the prologue to the Jew of Malta. "We pursue the story of a rich and famous Jew who lived in Malta: you shall find him still, in all his projects, a sound Machiavil; and that's his character." As for the popularity of the Machiavellian monster, his spirit did not brood over Marlowe's tragedy only[1], for he was quite familiar to the Elizabethan playgoer from the time of Kyd and Marlowe[2]. Let us return to the Jew's devilish character. Over the caricature in the Forest Roll of Essex we find the concise but clear description, Aaron, son of the Devil, fil diaboli, and the following quotations from *The Merchant of Venice* which fairly correspond with Chaucer's opinion, show that the character of the Jew had become firmly fixed in the course of the ages. "Certainly the Jew is the very devil incarnal" (*Merchant of Venice* II, II, 24). "Let me say 'amen' betimes lest the devil cross my prayer, for here he comes in the

---

[1] Boas, *Shakespeare and his Predecessors*, p. 50.
[2] *Cambridge History of English Literature*, Vol. VI, p. 167, and also Macaulay.

likeness of a Jew" and when Tubal enters Salanio says "here comes another of the tribe: a third cannot be matched, unless the devil himself turn Jew".

Throughout literature the New Testamentary cruelty runs parallel with the New Testamentary hatred and we have seen how all evil spirits, inclusive of the Arch-fiend, their master, find it convenient to take up their abode in the body of the Jew to torment the innocent Christians, as they did Jesus. So it is quite natural that "in Venice towne not long agoe, a *cruell* Iew did dwell". In *The Jew of Malta*, Act II, Barabas first teaches Ithamore "be thou void of these affections, compassion, love, vain hope, and heartless fear, be moved at nothing, see thou pity none" .... etc. "As for myself, I walk abroad o'nights, and kill sick people groaning under walls;" and then follow twenty-five lines containing cruelties the least of which would make any respectable man shudder. The cruelties of the Jew in *A Christian turned Turk* remind us of *The Jew of Malta*[1]. The Jew's daughter is an equally amiable creature. Having killed poor Hugh, "Scho laid him on a dressing borde, and drest him like a swine", "and laughing said, Gae nou and pley with zour sweet play-feres nine."

We have revealed the Jew's soul and shown its demoniacal qualities. Let us now bring some details of his character to the fore. The spirit of good is a fusing spirit, it knits the human hearts together, it is a unifying power and its name might be altruism. So we need not be greatly astonished at finding the Jew an egoist. This trait of character is best expressed by Barabas, when he simply declares, "so I live, perish

[1] Daborne, *A Christian turned Turk*, ed. by Prof. Dr. A. E. H. Swaen.

all the world". Even his daughter he loves (as far as a Jew void of natural affections can love) from a purely egoistical point of view, for when Abigail is no longer the daughter of his soul, she becomes a perfect stranger to him and an enemy that must be extirpated. That this trait is pure imagination need not be emphasized. The tribal unity of the Jews and their tender domestic life are too well known to require any refutation of this calumny, besides literature itself admits these qualities in spite of its obvious intention to hide them, as I shall show later on.

His Aim in Life and Mode of Living. — In what direction does this base egoistical soul move, what is its aim and purpose? In reply to this we expect some spiritual ideal. But we are deceived in our expectation. In spite of the fact that we know the Jews to be believers in the ethical development and perfection of mankind through their religion, in spite of the fact that we know the Jews to have been held together by this their common ideal, which showed them the final salvation of mankind, in spite of the fact that they have retained this ideal under the most trying circumstances, and in spite of the fact that this idealism has kept the Jewish race intact, in spite of all these things older literature has shown us the Jew as void of all idealism, as a gross groveling materialist, in fulfilment no doubt of the Gospel which accused him of covetousness. If we compare the Jew with the Christian hero of *The Merchant of Venice* we almost fancy we see a Morality, in which Antonio represents a faint reflection of Jesus, a Christian Gentleman with lofty ideals. The Jew's head, however, is full of money-matters, he has only material interests, he is bent on business, his thoughts are businesslike. This may be partly in accordance with truth and Mammon maybe a faint reflexion of what a Jew seemed to be; but a man is a mixture of all or nearly all human peculiarities and the figures of a Morality would be absurdities in real life.

In literature the Jew strikes us as morose and stern, he is never really gay. Thus for instance all gaiety in *The Merchant of Venice* is reserved for the Christians. It is quite possible that the Jews struck the Christians like this, and it may be that this made Shakespeare say that the Jew's house was dull. But this like the previous and other absurdities about the Jews was based upon a superficial knowledge of the Jew. The Jew in reality was neither morose nor stern, Jewish fun and humour are almost racial qualities and his house was certainly not dull. The Jew no doubt found his sole pleasure and gaiety at home. When his house had a gloomy or dull aspect, its inside was bright with the many lights that were kindled on Sabbath's eve and shone upon the good things that were produced and vied with the smiles that played on the faces of the parents. The Christians, however, though they were familiar with domestic felicity, set greater store by the open air pleasures in which they could freely indulge. The tilt-yard, the marketplace, the theatre, the taverns and the streets saw no jousting, fighting, playing, drinking, singing Jews. This jolly, sunny side of life appealed also to the dramatists who naturally excluded the Jew from it, but nevertheless blundered by representing him as a morose, stern or dull creature. The composers of the religious drama had seen a somewhat different Jew,

a Jew who could laugh and dance, but this Jew's
mirth was wickedness as it was no innocent outcome
of gladness of the heart, but malicious joy at the
sufferings of the Lord.

Jewish Criminality. — Nobody will be surprised
that a creature gifted with a Jewish soul will be a criminal and that the character of his criminality will differ
from that of an English criminal. There is robust
undisguised brutality in the Christian robber, he has
a certain frankness about him and the lusty fighting
in which the ruffian indulges, when he wants to achieve
his purpose, has something quite sympathetic. The
Jew's crimes, however, are not surrounded by an
open air atmosphere, there is something close and
oppressive about them. It will not do to call him a
coward, although this is often done and Benwash
shows himself one by creeping under the table, when his
visitors fall out and come to blows. His roundabout
ways, that indirectness has not got our sympathy.
There is a sheer lack of physical boldness which, though
it is not cowardice, yet makes the impression of it.
He does everything on the sly, never goes straight to
his purpose. Trapping, ensnaring, deception, over-
reaching or fooling are his means. The Jew not only
wants to satisfy his criminal cravings, but at the same
time desires to pass for an innocent harmless creature
and to achieve this he is represented as working with
the greatest subtlety. I may as well mention in passing
that the Jew's criminality in literature is generally
based upon a spirit of revenge that is said to dominate
him. It is recorded that in 1211 no less than 300 rabbis
of France and England started for a pilgrimage to the

Holy Land [1], that the Jews in York rather immolated themselves than surrender and that Jews have ever shown the greatest heroism in their hopeless struggle against their religious prosecutors, yet the fact that they were considered as cowards strikes me less than that they were said to be dominated by a spirit of revenge. The greatest trait of character that has helped the Jew to hold out against his enemies and in some respects made him gain the victory, is his yielding nature, again an almost racial characteristic. If he had returned the moral and physical blows, if he had indulged a desire for revenge he would have been no more and therefore all this revenge-nonsense is merely invented to justify the wrongs heaped upon the Jew, a rather topsy-turvy manner but artistically conceived all the same.

When speaking about the Jew's character as criminal, I ought to have mentioned his propensity to betray, which Judas bequeathed to Barabas, a propensity quite in keeping with his general character and the most detestable in the eyes of the Christians, but which, is only based on the Gospel. To make a long matter short, all impulses that actuate the Jew are only evil ones. He is an equivocator and a liar, a heartless assassin, a devil and a coward. That soul and character of the Jew, as revealed by early English literature, are purely artistic conceptions will not be disputed by anyone that lays claim to a sane mind, for if a hundredth part of all the nonsense about it were true, not a single

---

[1] I mention this, as I think no Jewish coward would venture through Christian countries upon such a hard journey, the purpose of which was merely to satisfy his love of the Holy Land.

Jew would have been left on the face of the earth.

His Intellect and Learning. — We have now reconstructed the Jew, making use of the materials supplied by literature for his outward appearance, we have supplied him with a soul, a motive power again borrowed from literature, but we have not yet drawn attention to the third requirement without which a human creature cannot be imagined; we have not yet drawn attention to the Jew's mental qualities, his intellect and learning. In the Encyclopædia Britannica we find that in medieval Europe, literature and affairs, science and statecraft, poetry and medicine, these various expressions of human nature and activity were so harmoniously balanced that they might be found in the possession of one and the same individual, and that individual a Jew! Craik in his *Manual of English Literature* speaks of the numbers of learned Jews that were everywhere to be found. In England the Jews had schools in London, York, Lincoln, Lynn, Norwich Oxford, Cambridge and other towns, which appear to have been attended by Christians as well as by Jews. Some of these seminaries, indeed, were colleges rather than schools. Besides the Hebrew and Arabic languages, arithmetic and medicine are mentioned among the branches of knowledge that were taught in them. Besides, it should be known that among the Jews study has been considered a chief virtue from the very earliest time, just as chivalry was the chief virtue of the Anglo-Saxons and Normans. In fact their love of study is based on their racial peculiarities. The Jew's love of books can be traced to very early times.

Stokes [1] records manuscripts and documents possessed
by the Jews in England before the expulsion. From
these manuscripts it appears they did not restrict
themselves to Hebrew. In the Library of Trinity
College, Cambridge, there is a Psalterium Hebraico-
Latinum, numbered 782 in the catalogue. The Jews
as money-lenders also had as pledges books of different
nature [2] and I do not think it far-fetched to suggest
that those among them who had a turn for reading will
have availed themselves of the opportunity of increasing
their stock of knowledge. Thus, for instance, in 1278
there was a lawsuit about a pledge of St. Paul's
Epistles, St. Matthew, etc. No doubt the Jewish scholar
wanted to know their contents when he was challenged
to that mental contest 'the disputation' which I have
already mentioned. There is a curious entry in the
Rolls in the year 1279, which states that the poor
students of Oxford had pawned so many of their books
with the Jews that they could not go on with their
studies. And I think that these and other unredeemed
pledges helped to form the libraries which were found
in the Jew's possession at their expulsion. A Jew at
Oxford being converted to the Christian faith, sued
for the moiety of his goods and had them delivered
according to the following schedule, which shews that
he was a man of learning: one book of notable Con-
stitution; one Graecism (Greek Grammar?); one Le-
gend(?); one large Doctrinal; etc. Then mention is
made of manuscripts containing commentaries and

---

[1] *Transactions Jewish Historical Society*, Vol. VIII, pp. VII—19 and 78.
[2] Perhaps it is not merely accidental that even nowadays there are so many
Jewish second hand book-sellers.

histories, for instance by Josephus, i.e. Josippon between 1141 and 1180. Aesops Fables were also translated into Hebrew [1]. We find in *La Revue des Etudes Juives*, IV, pp. 255. Le Ms. B. N. fr. 1, qui date du commencement du XIVe siècle et contient une traduction de la Bible en dialecte Anglo-Normand, renferme aux fo[s] 258vo et 259ro, à la suite des Lamentations de Jérémie, un alphabet dans lequel chaque lettre hébraïque est expliquée par un mot Latin et par le mot anglais correspondant. Just as the chivalrous knight took great care that his virtues passed on to his children, the Jewish scholar took great care that his learning passed on to his son and education has always been one of their great cares. So G. Friedlander in 'Shakespeare and the Jew' (page 2) has some ground to say that it was the Jew who kept the torch of knowledge aflame throughout the dark period of the Middle Ages.

Let us now turn from the Jew in History to the Jew in Literature. In whatever way he may be represented there, stupidity is not one of his traits. Of course we need not expect that he is complimented on account of his mental capacities, as this would not be in keeping with his general treatment and against the Gospel which calls him void of understanding and therefore his insight is called slyness, his understanding is stigmatized as cunning. And yet there are numbers of passages from which we may conclude that his considerable mental powers were unconsciously admitted. To start with, Barabas is possessed of books, which must not be considered of little importance, for he is acquainted with their contents, from which we must conclude

[1] *Jewish Quarterly Rev.*, pp. 533.

that he was a scholar. This is confirmed by the fact that Barabas speaks various languages or at any rate seems to be acquainted will them, as Latin, Italian, Spanish, French and no doubt Hebrew. Nor are these all the accomplishments he has acquired, for he has studied medicine in Italy or to use his own words, "being young I studied physic and began to practise first upon the Italian. There I enriched the priests with burials". He prepares sleeping-draughts and poison. Finally, if successful trading is something more than mere luck or fortune, if it requires keenness of perception, insight, intellect and promptitude of action in some, or diligence, unfagging effort and ambition in others, then we must expect these qualities in a Barabas or a Shylock, although the dramatist does not expressly state them.

Owing to their mental qualities the Jewish doctors acquired great skill in the art of healing and on account of this they were often appointed physicians to noble persons. Thus Queen Elisabeth had a physician, Lopez, of Jewish descent, who was tried and executed in 1594 (Lopez was probably innocent of the crime he was charged with, an attempt at poisoning the Queen, for which see Friedlander, page 18 and *The Cambridge Modern History*, Vol. III, page 335). In passing we may add that this Lopez spoke five European languages [1]. History tells us that the Jew studied medicine and thus applied his intellect to a good purpose; therefore literature must needs make him the poisoner par excellence. Thus for instance in Selimus the cunning Jew, Abraham the court physician, professes physic

---

[1] Lee, *Original of Shylock.*

and is well versed in poisons. Barabas revels in their use. Francisco the treacherous favourite of the Duke of Millaine [1], in the play of this name, enters the ducal palace in the disguise of a Jewish doctor and covers the lips and hands of the corpse of Marcelia with poisonous paint, so that Sforza is killed by kissing her. So we see that in literature the good mental qualities of the Jew are turned into wickedness by misapplication, which is again quite in keeping with his inferior soul. The Jew's propensity to poison must be traced back to the Black Death (1348), or to the Great Pestilence (1320) as already explained. In Trevisa's translation of Higden's *Polychronicon* (Rolls Series) VI, 385, we find that Charles Grossus was i-poisond of a Iew' in 1387 [2].

We often come across passages in which the Jew is called proud and stubborn, and taking into consideration all that history tells us, I arrive at the conclusion that the Jew must have struck the Christian as such. They must certainly have been proud of their mental qualities, just as the Christian was proud of his valour, he must certainly have been stubborn in his refusal to give up his faith in exchange for another, when he considered that he owed his good qualities to his God, whose spirit and word were contained in this faith. Now our Jew is ready and the task of showing him in action is incumbent upon us, but first we must find out the fox's den, the Jew's home, first we want to make the acquaintance of his family, his life at home, his friends, and so on.

[1] Massinger, *Duke of Millaine*, see Cambridge History of English Literature.
[2] Another allusion we find in John Marston's *Malcontent* (1604), Mendoza: Canst thou impoison? Malevole: Excellently, no Jew, pothecary or politician better.

His House. — Let us take his house first. In the ballad of *The Jew's Daughter,* line 35, we read "And she (the murdered boy's mother) ran into the Jewis castel", an expression which I first took for an exaggeration, but which upon further investigation proved to be founded on history. Grætz in *Geschichte der Juden* speaking on this subject in King Henry the Second's time says, "Sie bewohnten die groszen Städte, und in London waren manche von ihnen zu solchen Reichthümern gelangt, dasz ihre Häuser sich wie Königliche Paläste ausnahmen[1])," and so also in York, with which compare what Green says: "His (the Jew's) own example gave a new direction to domestic architecture. The buildings which, as at Lincoln and St. Edmundsbury, still retain their title of 'Jews' houses' were almost the first houses of stone which superseded the mere hovels of the English burghers".

Such a Jew's house[2] had underground vaulted chambers then followed the groundfloor again vaulted and without windows. The principal dwelling room was on the first floor. The fire place was on the side towards the street, the chimney being corbelled out over the door, the lower part of it, with corbels forming a sort of canopy over the doorway. This was richly decorated. Some of the windows were good Norman ones of two lights, with a staff between. The staircase seems to have been internal. Fancy such a house with strong walls and a tiled roof situated on a steep hill[2]) and the word castle is no longer inappropriate. For like

[1] Barab.: "I have bought a house as great and fair as is the Governor's. (Jew of Malta, p. 181.)

[2] *Jewish Quarterly Review,* Vol. V, in which J. Jacobs quotes Turner's *Domestic Architecture,* pp. 7, 41.

a castle it served two purposes, housing its master and his family and protecting him against the frequent attacks to which he was subjected. The underground chambers, the absence of windows on the groundfloor, the tiled roof, the thick walls and may be its situation were meant for defence. This unsafety and even attacks are reflected in literature. Shylock's anxiety in this respect when he hears that there are going to be masques, is obvious, and the houses of Barabas and Benwash are actually visited by burglars. When the Jews were expelled their houses passed into the hands of their prosecutors and some of these houses still exist. The house in which Barabas lives is so large that it is fit to be converted into a nunnery and will harbour many nuns. It is distinctly spoken of as a goodly house. Nor does Benwash live in an inferior style, for his house is described as 'noblemanlike' with 'great windowes and a little wicket' and it has some outhouses. Taking into consideration the insecurity he was permanently in, the Jew was undoubtedly unable to exercise the virtue of hospitality in his house. Its strongness, seclusion and the character of its inhabitants will no doubt have surrounded it with an air of horror and mystery. No doubt the Jews, if they had no synagogue, will have come together to pray, and the Jews pray aloud, so here was an additional uncanniness about these houses, from which those strange sounds emanated. Many a time the Christians will have wondered what was happening in that house into which nobody could peep. Was a cruel black Jewess killing an innocent fair-haired Christian boy, or were a number of Jews crucifying him? Were they gathered

round a table upon which the poor victim lay stretched
out and waiting for the cruel circumcising or emascu-
lating knife, or were they obliging their Christian
nurses to milk themselves into privies for three days
after receiving sacrament, lest it should be infused into
their children with her milk[1]). And the wealth these
houses contained, the untold wealth! So much about
these possibilities, which are rather thrilling. Very
likely a great part of the house was arranged as an office,
shop and warehouse, but of greater importance than
the arrangement of the house are its inmates, the Jew's
wife, his sons and daughters and his servants.

His Family. — In history family life among the
Jews has always been praised, but in literature no
such thing! Where are conjugal harmony, domestic
peace, filial tenderness, where the pure life and love at
home, spoken of by historians? [2] They are nowhere to
be found in literature! Maternity with all its sweetness
has no place in it, nay is not even hinted at. The Christian Mathias has a tender, loving mother, but Barabas
must convey to the reader or spectator the idea of
Jewish paternity. As for conjugal affection, the only
line that hints at something of this nature is l. 102 of
Act III. Sc. 1. (*Merchant of Venice*). When Tubal tells
Shylock about a ring Jessica gave for a monkey, Shylock bursts out: "Thou torturest me, Tubal: it was my
turquoise; I had it of Leah, when I was a bachelor: I
would not have given it for a wilderness of monkeys".
The cry of the lonely Jew may betray some burning
emotion at the loss of the jewel which reminded him of

[1] Toovey, *Anglia Judaica*, Oxford, 1738, p. 104.
[2] See also *Enc. Britt.*, page 405. Vol. 15.

the dear girl that had become his wife and stood by him in the vicissitudes of life. But an other explanation is more likely, namely that Shakespeare simply wanted to show the baseness of Shylock's character, that it was only the turquoise of which he regretted the loss, for turquoises were held in high esteem on account of their secret powers.

When Shylock hears Gratiano say, he would his wife were in heaven, that is, dead, so she could entreat some power to change the currish Jew's mind, he says *aside* and it is this 'aside' that gives a ring of truth to his words, "these be the Christian husbands. I have daughter; would any of the stock of Barabas had been her husband rather than a Christian." These words certainly betray conjugal affection.

Another allusion to Jewish matrimony we find in *A Christian turned Turk*, where Benwash declares, we are not Italianate to lock up our women, we set them free, give open entertainment." But lest the reader should think that we have here an instance of early emancipation of women, I hasten to add that this is mentioned only to cast a slur upon Jewish family life, for Benwash uses his wife as a decoy to draw in trade[1]. As Benwash's wife is not a Jewess but a Turkish woman, I do not think it necessary to dwell upon her harlotry with a Christian. But it is one more blow in the Jew's face that in the only instance, where we find him possessed of a wife, this wife should be a mere whore.

---

[1] With which compare Barabas' instructing his daughter: "Entertain Lodowick, with all the courtesy you can afford, provided you keep your maidenhead, dissemble, swear, protest, vow love to him, kiss him. See also page 126 as regards Lupo, his daughter and Volpone.

To this notable absence of Jewish wives must be added the equally notable absence of sons. This, of course enhances and brings to the fore the principal characters, who greatly filled the mind of the audience, the popular or rather impopular Jew and his beautiful daughter, the latter, to be sure, richly adorned with jewelry. An old father and young beautiful daughter, what touching pages literature has devoted to this group! But for the Jew and Jewess there was no place in those pages. Barabas loves his daughter, he holds her dear, he says (Act. I), "nay, let 'em combat, conquer, and kili all, so they spare me, my daughter, and my wealth"! Yet he teaches her to lie and deceive and in the end finds it in his heart to poison her, his lovely, his only child, who was a sweet child too, as appears from the play and she a girl of scarce fourteen years of age, a mere child. A somewhat more human father Shakespeare makes of Shylock. To start with, Shakespeare shows Jessica to be her father's enemy, so all the more insight in human nature is shown by making Shylock lament her elopement all the same. He wishes her dead at his foot (III, 1.73), but this wish does not seem to have a ring of truth. Whether Shakespeare really wanted this passage to be understood in this way, however, is not at all sure, for the addition of "and the jewels in het ear!" takes away some of the sincerity of his lament.

Let us turn for a little while from the Jew and devote our sole attention to his daughter, the Jewess, in literature. Let us not be squeamish, the Jew was an object of *hatred* and the Jewess of *lust*. For this and nothing else explains her being represented in a way almost

the reverse of the manner in which the Jew is treated,
with one notable exception, which we shall treat
first. A true Jew's daughter, one worthy of the blood
of Gernutus, Barabas or Shylock, is she of the Scottish
ballad. She is called the Jew's Daughter and not the
Jewess ,as the former name links her more directly with
the *Jew*. In fact, if the author had made a Jew the
hero of the ballad, it would not have differed much.
There is not much of a woman about the heroine, there
is not even much humanity about her, not the least
redeeming point in her vile behaviour, sheer cruelty
is the pivot upon which the story of the ballad turns.
How are we then to explain the quite different manner
in which Barabas's daughter Abigail or Jessica are
treated? What was the desert of the Jewish girl, what
her merits, that the artists showed her in quite an
amiable light. What was this inclination towards the
Jewesses based upon? Let us see. Benwash fears that,
if he had remained a Jew, his wife would have been
violated by Christians and Mahometans. This seems to
imply that such violations were not at all rare. Indeed,
when Volpone was drunk, he begot bastards on Gyp-
sies, *Jews* and black-moors [1]. What are we to think of
the following quotations? When Abigail dies, she says
".... and witness that I die a Christian [Dies]. Friar
Barn.: Ay, and a virgin too; *that* grieves me most. (*Jew
of Malta*). In Act I Mathias (on hearing that Abigail
has become a nun): ".... she were fitter for a tale of
love.... and better would she far become a bed, embraced in friendly lover's arm...." And when Lodowick declares his love for Abigail to Barabas, it is quite

[1] Ben Jonson, *Volpone*, p. 417 (Everyman's Ed.)

clear that no *marriage* is meant. Indeed Barabas says:
"I know your lordship would disdain *to marry* with the
daughter of a Jew". That Barabas should thus offer his
daughter is nothing strange. Ben Jonson in *The Fox* tells
us that signior Lupo, the physician, offered his daughter
to Volpone for a similar purpose[1]. It is perhaps this
passionate inclination towards beautiful Jewesses that
explains why Shakespeare [2] could make Lorenzo marry
Jessica, and Marlowe give Abigail two Christian lovers,
one of whom no less a gentlemen than Lodowick, the
son of the Governor of Malta. Far from being a creature
belonging to the realms of malicious fancy, Marlowe's
Abigail is a girl belonging more to a poet's loving imagination. Although somewhat weakly drawn, we see in
her quite a sympathetic girl, with, natural affections
and touching simplicity. She is described as an obe-
dient child, except in matters of love, her heart she
cannot command, she sincerely loves the Christian
Mathias. Barabas makes his daughter an unwilling tool
in his murderous career. No wonder that she arrives
at the conclusion that there is no pity in Jews. It was
probably the artist's intention to show her so white a
creature, that the Jew might appear all the blacker.
If there had been Jewish nunneries, Abigail, weary
of the world, would have found a retreat there, but
her going to a Christian nunnery is a bit of a psychological puzzle, as there is no single instance that any of
the Christians with whom she conversed, tried to show
her by word or example anything of the superiority

---

[1] p. 433.
[2] The Church did not favour intermarriage and I think that Shakespeare
was a good son of hers in this respect, for he shows Jessica as a base woman.

of their faith. When dying, poisoned by her father, her last words express her hope that her father's soul may be saved.

Strange to say, however, domestic affections are here and there seen shimmering through in spite of the artists' attempts at hiding them. Combine for a single moment Shylock and Abigail and a possibility of love between these two flames up with brightening flame. This, however, would not have served the artists' purpose and Jessica was added to Shylock.

Shylock's Jessica has quite a different character. Without such good reasons as Abigail she behaves more like an enemy of Shylock. Her reasons for doing so contradict what history says about Jewish family-life. "Our house is hell" (II, 3, 2) and one line further she speaks of its tediousness and some lines farther again "though I am a daughter to his blood, I am not to his manners." Abigail is a simple girl, Jessica is full of guile and duplicity. She lies to her father (II. 5. 44), she robs her father's gold and jewels (II, 4, 31) and even betrays him [1] (III, 2, 280) so that her words in II, 3. 14.: "Alack, what heinous sin is it in me to be ashamed to be my father's child!" are some what out of keeping with her character. On the whole I must say that there is nothing specially Jewish about either Abigail or Jessica. They may belong to any race and to any religion. No trace of any conflict of thoughts or feeling when Jessica gives up her religion and social surroundings. Here again Abigail is shown to better advantage, for she is first averse to becoming a novice and only turns Christian, when she discovers her father's real

[1] Abigail would not betray her father in spite of all.

character. They both love Christians, as if this were
quite a matter of course. This then is all the Jew's
family, no wife, no son, only a daughter that serves
more or less as a foil to his glaring wickedness.

His Servants. — Most Jews in the drama are represented as having a servant, and in a way we may say,
like master like man. The Jew and his servant constantly
remind me of the Devil and the Vice of the old miracles
and are no doubt their successors. The Devil is the Jew
and his servant is the Vice, that is to say the buffoon,
the wag, the jester, the mocker as circumstances
may require.

Dodypoll has his servant Zaccharee, then we have
the pestering servant of Mammon with the great
fiery nose, then Launcelot, Ithamore and Rabshake;
their only real occupation seems to be to tease, plague
and pester their masters and in doing so amuse the
audience. In Rabshake this is especially odious as he
himself is a Jew, a striking Jew; he has more Jewish
traits of character than any of the other Jews, Shylock
perhaps excepted; he is full of that certain peculiar
sort of Jewish fun which the Jews highly appreciate
amongst themselves. Launcelot grumbles at his being
famished in Shylock's service; you may tell every
finger he has with his ribs (notice the silly joke), but
Shylock says "thou shalt not gormandise, (with his
new master) as thou hast done with me, and sleep and
snore, and rend apparel out." Whether the master or
his servant is right does not appear from the play, but
I suppose we must take for granted that Launcelot tells
no lie in this respect. The Jewish laws, however, concerning the treatment of slaves reveal most humane

principles and though Launcelot is not exactly a slave, there is no single reason to suppose that Jewish masters excelled in maltreating their domestic servants. Besides Shylock says of Launcelot "the patch is kind enough" and such words do not sound well in the mouth of a harsh master.

These servants have in common a perfect absence of any esteem or affection for their masters and are generally possessed of a malicious joy at their misfortunes, they are all half fool, half knave and of a comic character.

His Friends. — Nor is the Jew any more fortunate in his friends. Birds of a feather flock together is a law in nature, and in the history of man, prosecution has always acted as glue in this respect. Groups of persons joined by common principles, on account of which they are prosecuted, have always shown signs of the greatest mutual loyalty. In this respect the Jew, the most prosecuted creature that ever was, must of course form an exception in literature and yet in spite of the artists' intention proofs of their close tribal union crop up here and there [1]). In literature the Jew could be no faithful friend not even to a Jew, thus Barabas, after expressing his greatest indifference as to the weal and woe of his co-religionists, winds up his soliloquy by saying "Ego mihimet sum semper proximus" (Act. I). Nor is there much love lost between Shylock and his friend Tubal, who can only coldly comfort him by repeating the rumours about his daughter's

---

[1] John Gower's Jew, however, says that he is free to deceive and rob anybody "bot if he be withoute drede A verrai Jew as am I". Langland also pointed out their readiness to help each other.

throwing away money in Genoa, and bartering away
a ring of great value for a monkey and yet Shylock's
dignified claim on behalf of his race to be treated as
men and his strong tribal sentiment glimmer beneath
the coating of tarnish with which the artist has be-
smeared him.

His Philanthropy. — In literature little love is lost
between the Jew and his friends, less between him and his
servants and no love at all between him and man in general. Let us turn to the Old Testament, the book grown out
of the heart and head of the Jewish people, for information
on this point. "The stranger that sojourneth with you shall
be unto you as the home-born among you and thou shalt
love him as thyself; for ye were sojourners in the land
of Egypt" (Leviticus 19. 34). This law tells us an other
tale about the spirit of the Jew than is found in Gernutus. "Gernutus called was the Jew, which never
thought to die: nor never yet did any good, to them in
streets that lie". The slightest acquaintance with the
biblical laws regarding the poor non-Jews would be an
antidote against this poisonons lie, or this in the Jew of
Malta: "the Jewish faith, hard-hearted to the poor". (Act.
IV). When Rutilio, in *The Custom of the Country*, is cast
ashore (act. II, Sc. 1), he dare not hope the Jew will
help him in his need "because you are a Jew Sir, and
courtesies come sooner from the Devil than any of
your nation", to which Zabulon answers: "we are men,
and have like you compassion, when we find fit subjects for our bounty." This Jewish assertion is corrob-
orated by a fact, for when Sir Thomas Sherley was
imprisoned at Constantinople, he was befriended by a
kindhearted Jewish merchant. This kindness was duly

rewarded by literature by enriching the number of wicked Jews in Art with the personality of Zariph, a raving, human-flesh-eating demon. Hallibeck (*Custom of the Country*) calls the Jewish heart "relentlesse as a flint". Raymond (in *A Christian turned Turk*) calls the Jew "hard-hearted" and later on speaks of his "marble heart". Antonio (*Merch. of Venice*, V, I, 69/82) says that the hardest thing of all is a Jewish heart, and when the Duke (*Merch. of Venice* IV, I, 3) calls Shylock " a stony adversary, an inhuman wretch uncapable of pity, void and empty from any dram of mercy", I do not think he looked upon this Jew as a law-abiding Hebrew, nor had the well-known philanthropy of the modern Jew evidently dawned in English literature. There is a striking unanimity in the chorus of voices denouncing the Jew's hard heart of which the oldest example is found in Ælefric and which is based upon the New Testament description of it.

His Religion. — We spoke about the Old Testament and thus we touched the Jew's religion. Let us see what history says on this point. "French Judaism [1] was thus in a sense more human if less humane than that of the Spanish variety; the latter produced thinkers, statesmen, poets and scientists, the former, men of robuster because of more naïve and concentrated piety. In Spain and North Africa persecution created that strange and significant phenomenon maranism or crypto-Judaism, a public acceptance of Islam or Christianity combined with a private fidelity to the rites of Judaism. But in England, France and Germany persecution altogether failed to shake the courage of

[1] *Enc. Britt.* Vol. 15, p. 405.

the Jews, and martyrdom was borne in preference to ostensible apostasy. The third crusade, famous for the participation of Richard I, was occasion for bloody riots in England, especially in York, where 150 Jews immolated themselves *to escape baptism*." And what does literature make of the Jew's religion[1]? Benwash turns Turk for no nobler reason than to keep his bed free from these Mahometan Dogges. Yet, when he died, he called out: "Beare witnesse, though I liu'd a Turke I dye a Jew (p. 252), from which I conclude that he felt some qualms of conscience at his apostasy, which he did not feel, however, when the thought of death was far from him, for then his opinion was "Christian or Turk you are more wise, I know, than with religion to confine your hope." In *The Jew of Malta* Machiavel says: "I count religion but a childish toy and hold there is no sin but ignorance", and Machiavel says that the Jew favours him. Once a year at least a Jew prays in his *shrouds* and yet we read: "Gernutus called was the Jew which never thought to die". Barabas (Act. I) had a very practical use for religion for it "hides many mischiefs from suspicion", and although Shylock says in accordance with the Jewish laws that he will not eat and drink with Christians, yet we find in Act II, Sc. V, 11,: "I am bid forth to supper.... I'll go in hate, to *feed* upon the prodigal Christian. In Act III, Sc. I, line 110 Shakespeare makes

---

[1] Although all Jews are represented as proud of their religion, there is only one instance where this pride is spoken of in somewhat appreciating manner, see page 45, but this is only done to make the final conversion all the more glorious. Nevertheless it betrays the true mentality of the Jew, which in spite of everything is traceable in nearly all Jews of Literature, a spirit of staunch adherence to ideals.

Shylock say: "Go, Tubal, fee me an officer.... I will have the heart of him.... Go, go, Tubal, and meet me at our Synagogue." Shakespeare probably intended to add another shade of darkness to the character of Shylock, by making him still devout, while meditating his horrible vengeance. This vengeance itself is against the Jewish law and Friedlander traces its Roman character.

On the whole a number of glaring blunders show that the Jews' religion, if observed at all is done so in a very superficial and uncritical manner [1]. The Jews sometimes swear by Mohamed, so we see that they are confounded with the Turks, who were likewise considered as the enemies of the Christians. This mistake together with some that I have already mentioned proceed from ignorance. Here follows one that is based on wilful contortion. John Gower, namely makes the Jew openly avow: "I am a Jew, and bi *mi lawe* I shal to no man be felawe to kepe him trowthe in word ne dede, bot if he be withoute drede a verrai Jew as am I". So this would inply that the Jewish laws command the Jew to deceive all, except his co-religionists. The Jews were the first people that believed in one God and made that one God and what they called his teaching the basis of their social, domestic and individual life. Upon his teaching they have built up a spiritual treasure house in the shape of their literature, the reflection of their culture. So we see that their God is warp and woof of their spiritual being. How strange it must therefore seem to an unprejudiced reader to see how the Jew's religion has been degraded to a tattered masquerade cloak and

[1] See also pages 77, 78.

his God to a hidden idol, only to be taken out on rare occasions. If literature had been true to history, the Jew would have been represented as a man earnestly striving to live up to the moral instruction laid down in the Old Testament and holding communion with his God under all circumstances of life, thanking Him in moments of bliss and humbly beseeching Him to remove his guilt in years of affliction.

I now must draw attention to a ridiculous contradiction. While older literature is constantly harping upon the same string, that religious sentiment and awe of God are looked for in vain with the Jew, he is constantly represented as averse to baptism. This simply means that the Christian authors were acquainted with the historical fact that the Jews were faithful to their God and his laws, that they knew the Jewish martyrs and simply would not, or rather could not, understand and admit the awful religious sentiment that possessed them. Although matters have considerably changed in this respect, we may confidently say that, when the name Jew is mentioned, it is as a rule inextricably connected with the idea of religion. For the sake of religion the Jews suffered all that a race of human beings can undergo, and yet we find this faithful adherence to their God and his laws[1] ridiculed, turned into hypocrisy or denied altogether in Literature. There he has only one God, and that God is 'Mammon'.

Money. — Mammon, this name leads us on to the Jew's money. Just as much as a Jew must needs be provided with a hooked proboscis, the money-bags form an

---

[1] Benwash swears by Abraham's dust and the Holy Writ and breaks these oaths.

inseparable feature of the seed of Abraham. It is true, they are not carried about so prominently as their noses, yet in some mysterious way we are always aware of them. They take hold of the reader's imagination. Money! The Jew's keen brains are always thinking of it, his sharp eyes are always looking for it, and his claw-like hands are always grasping it. When his mind is bent on its acquisition, he assumes an attitude that strongly reminds one of the vulture in his cage at the Zoo, when the keeper approaches with carrion food. Money! He loves it for its own sake. He does not love it for the same reason, why most Christians are fond of it, not because it gives a feeling of certainty, independence, not because it is the key to spiritual and material pleasure, but simply because it is money. In fact we might almost say that money is elevated by the Jew into something like a God, a veritable Mammon or Gold Calf and although there is something paradoxical in it, the adoration (especially by Barabas) has a vein of idealism and the laying up of treasure is, in the eyes of Barabas, sanctified by divine benediction. Barabas's ideal of life is (Act I) to "inclose infinite riches in a little room." Of course it need not be stated expressly that the Jew always hid his money. In illustration of the above. I adduce some quotations from the prologue to *The Jew of Malta* pronounced by Machiavel .... "the tragedy of a Jew, who smiles to see how full his bags are crammed: which money was not got without my means". Especially instructive in this respect is the effective scene in the first act, where Barabas is discovered with heaps of gold before him in his counting-house. Speaking of his riches he says: "these are the

blessings promised to the Jews, and herein was old
Abraham's happeness". The Jew's desire for money
is considered as a proof of base material inclination
and of his lack of a high spiritual aim. Judas must
have been infected with this craving, when he sold
his beloved Lord, when he abandoned his soul's bliss for
a paltry thirty pieces of silver. We all know that the
blessing promised to the Jews and Abraham's happiness
was, that their offspring would be numerous as the
sands of the sea. Children are the greatest blessing of
the Jews. I wonder therefore, whether it is accidentally
or on purpose that both Marlowe and Shakespeare
connect children and gold. When Barabas recovers his
money, he is mad with joy and calls out: "O my girl,
my gold", when Shylock is mad with grief at the loss
of both his child and his treasure he exclaims "my
daughter, o my ducats", when their money is taken
from them, both Barabbas and Shylock, declare that
money is dearer than life (*Jew of Malta* Act I and
Merchant of Venice, Act IV. Sc. I, l. 370) and quite in
keeping with this is the fact that Barabas hugs his
bags and calls them his 'soul's sole hope'.

His occupation. — How did the Jews become possessed of great riches? Marlowe makes Machiavel say,
that their money was not got without his (Machiavel's)
means [1]. Let us just trace the Jew's occupation in
history. In Palestina he was originally a sturdy culti-
vator of the soil. Zollschan says that the Jewish laws
originally were inimical to commerce and usury.
Later on and out of their own country they are chiefly

---

[1] Latimer (*Remains*, ii p. 42) says, "all they that live on usury have their gains by the Devil".

merchants and as such play a prominent part in Europe. In the *Encyclopaedia Brittanica* I find "that in France under Charlemagne, the Jews who had begun to settle in Gaul in the time of Cæsar, were more than tolerated. They were allowed to hold land and were encouraged to become what their ubiquity qualified them to be — the merchant princes of Europe". This is, in fact, faithfully reflected in the first scene of *The Jew of Malta,* where Barabas congratulates himself upon his successful speculations in all parts of the world and boasts that he has Jewish correspondents in almost every country of Europe [1]. This ability as merchants also appears from the following quotation from Toovey "these encouragements (in the time of Henry III) causing fresh numbers of them to come hither daily from foreign parts, the people (!) soon began to find the inconvenience of it. For, as the Jews understood trade better than our own merchants (from the general correspondence they held with their brethren in all parts of the world, and from managing their traffick as it were by a common stock) they were able to undersell them; no one cared to buy anything of a Christian." Very soon the Jew's trade was hampered and frequently made impossible, whilst only usury was left to them, because this was thought to be unworthy of the Christians. In literature the greatest stress is laid upon the fact that the Jew was a moneylender in the first place. That the Jew is represented as a moneylender is, of course, not at all unfounded. Here follows a note to line 41, Act I, Sc. III in *The Merchant of Venice* giving information on this point. "Douce quotes from Thomas's

[1] Everyman's Library, p. 165.

History of Italy, 1561, fol. 76*b*: 'It is almoste incredyble what gaine the *Venetians* receive by the usury of the Jewes, both pryuately and in common. For in everye citee the Jewes kepe open shops of usurie, taking gaiges of ordinarie for. XV. in the hundred by the yere: and if at the yere ende, the gaige be not redemed, it is forfeite, or at the least dooen away to a great dis-advantage: by reason wherof the Jewes are out of measure wealthie in those parties". L. Kellner in the *Quelle von Marlowe's Jew of Malta* quotes Nicholas de Nicholay, who informs us about the Jews in the Levant, 'how they have practically monopolised all trade there. Besides, this detestable natioun of the Jews are men full of malice, fraud, deceit and subtil dealing, exercising execrable usuries amongst the Christian and other nations without consciousness or reprehension .... a thing which is great ruin to the country and people where they are conversant'. A similar state of affairs is found in *De universali et no-vissimi Judaeorum vocatione*, London, 1590, p. 33. Full of malice, fraud, deceit and subtil dealing, without conscience or reprehension. We hear the echo of the Gospel. As for their execrable usury, Latimer (*Remains* ii, p. 42) says: 'all they that live of usury, they have their gains by the devil' I mention all this to show that even usury, which is no doubt an outcome of the Jew's position in the Diaspora, is considered as an inherent propensity, already drawn attention to in the Gospel. There we find their covetousness mentioned as one of their peculiar vices. Having no spiritual interest, being no idealists, they are represented as brutal materialists. Gold is all they desire and they would like to grasp, if not all the treasure of the world, then at any rate as much as they possibly can or as Barabas says: "I have been zealous in the Jewish faith, hard-hearted to the poor, a covetous wretch, that would for lucre's sake have sold my soul; a hundred for a hundred I have ta'en; and now for store of wealth may I compare with all the Jews in Malta". Jew and usurer are practically synonymous in literature. The ballad, the song of the people, identifies them [1]). The first lines of Gernutus reflect the above: "In Venice towne not long agoe, a cruell Iew did dwell, which lived all on Usurie, as Italian writers tell". We need not observe that all is fearfully exaggerated and have no less an authority than Matthew Paris for the reverse, for he describes the Jewish usurers as fair and courteous men, whilst their Christian rivals are extortioners of the blackest kind. Here and there we find the Jews were otherwise occupied. Sometimes they are merchants and the article they deal in is mentioned. Thus Zariph, Barabas and Shylock buy and sell diamonds.. S. Lee tells us that in an anonymous piece published in 1609 (though probably written earlier) called *Every Woman in her Humour* a city wife suggests to a neighbour various means of obtaining a dress to enable her to go to court, and concludes the discussion with the words, "or if all fail, you may hire a good suit at a Jew's or broker's; it is a common thing, and especially among the common people" (Bullen's *Old Plays*, Vol. IV, p. 363) In *The Fox* by Ben Jonson, Sir Politick Would-Be says I .... took me a house, dealt with my Jews to furnish it with moveables —. That the above is no fancy

[1] Rollins, *A Pepysian Gárland*.

appears from the following quotation from Lee. "It is curious to note that Stowe, the contemporary historian of London (Shakespeare's time) states that Houndsditch was largely tenanted then, as now, by sellers of old apparel", but he complains that there had lately crept in among the old dwellers a number of pawnbrokers, a base kind of vermin, or rather, as St. Bernard thinks it more convenient to term them, baptisatos Judaeos, who take to themselves to be Christians". When we associate Stowe's words with that practice of hiring court suits at a Jew's mentioned by the dramatist, Elizabethan Houndsditch may fairly be credited with clothiers and pawnbrokers of Jewish origin. We find another allusion to Jews and their trade in Ben Jonson's *Every Man in His Humour*. "Why, Ned, I beseech thee, hast thou forsworn all thy friends in the Old Jewry? or dost thou think us all Jews that inhabit there? yet, if thou dost, come over, and but see our frippery; change an old shirt for a whole smock with us: do not conceive that antipathy between us and Hogsden, as was between Jews and hogs-flesh."

Then there are the Jewish doctors in literature. Lee traces some three doctors in Shakespeare's time. Besides the fame of the Jewish doctors went all over Europe and is restricted to no particular time. Popes and Christian legislators made use of their services. But soon the Church put a stop to this and in 1267 forbade the Christians to avail themselves of their skill commanding them to die rather than to be cured by persons whom she denounced as sorcerers. Of course it was no sorcery, that was at the bottom of it but religion and competition. Nevertheless the Jews continued to practise and Christians continued to make use of their experience. Before that time Richard I, though he was afraid of being bewitched by the Jews, is said to have invited a Jewish doctor and I have already mentioned the Jewish doctors of Henry IV and Sir Richard Whittington's wife. In literature, however, the doctor makes use of his skill for criminal purposes only.

The Jew never figures as a teacher of languages, nor as a student, and yet he must have been one of these, as many appear to have known Hebrew, Arabic, Greek, Latin, Italian, Spanish, French and English. Most probably Hebrew was taught at Oxford by Jewish scholars in Queen Elizabeth's time.

In *The Customs of the Country* and *A Christian turned Turk* the Jew is also a slave-dealer, bawd, pander and if needs be he also procures a murderer, a hired assassin. Of course he is a receiver of stolen goods and in one case he is a servant to a noble Lady (Zabulon to Hippolyta in *The Custom of the Country*) whose evil passions he must satisfy as a procurer.

Racial Hatred, Competition and Intolerance. — There are three principal reasons, why the Jew is hated in reality and these are reflected in literature. They are: difference of race, conflicting material interests or competition and difference of religion. As for racial differences, each race is apt to classify its own peculiarities as so many superior qualities, whereas, the peculiarities of the other race are generally misunderstood, misrepresented and put down as so many inferior qualities. This holds good physically and psychologically. A piece of white silk or velvet may make a beautiful impression, but a piece of black silk or velvet may make an equally beautiful impression. A white race however, considers its whiteness as something superior to the blackness of a black race. It must be put down to this phenomenon of short-sightedness and self-love in the human mind, that the Jew has been represented in the way we have described up till now. To this subtle and unobtrusive but nevertheless mighty cause for hatred must be added the gross and prominent and equally mighty one, namely the conflict of material interests or competition.

"The closer connexion between Europe and the East brought about by the crusades raised up a class of merchant traders among the Christians and from this time onwards restrictions on the sale of goods by Jews became frequent" [1]. If one reads the first act of *The Jew of Malta*, one cannot help being struck by the powerful description of the successful merchant and his extensive trade covering practically the whole of the then known world. The Jews were clever, suffering had made them so even more. If the law of the survival of the fittest be true, only those Jews had a chance that were keen enough to escape through the meshes of the net of persecution in which they were caught in the Middle Ages. Though they were driven about all over the world, it is wonderful but true that in spite of their sufferings they kept their eyes wide open and learned many things and saw many things which enabled them to practically master all European and Asiatic markets. Therefore there must

[1] *Enc. Britt.* Vol. 15, p. 405; Green's *Short Hist.* Ch. IV. Sec. V.

be truth in what Marlowe makes Barabas say about his enormous wealth, but equal truth lies in Barabas' words "Who hateth me but for my happiness?" (Act I). This jealousy and competition can be traced in more places. Thus in Act I. 3.40 Shylock says: "he (Antonio) lends out money gratis and brings down the rate of usance here with us in Venice" [1]. In fact Shylock and Antonio are both merchants and competitors. This is why Shylock (Act III Sc. I the end) says: "I will have the heart of him, if he forfeit; for, were he out of Venice, I can make what merchandise I will."

Having dealt with the instinctive racial hatred and the hatred arising from the struggle for life or competitive hatred, we now approach the intellectual hatred, which in the Middle Ages coalesced with religious hatred. The last reason then, but not the least, of the Christian hatred of the Jews, is that the latter murdered Jesus, wherefore, especially in early literature, they often figure as murderers of the Lord. Later on their murdering and crucifying propensity demonstrates itself in their cruel dealings with Christian children. Their hatred of Christ they show by blasphemy or by insulting the Cross. Thus we read in Toovey that a rich Jew named Abraham, the owner of a house and office in Wallingford, had in his possession an image of the Holy Virgin, which he most filthily defiled by covering it with excrements and which he likewise blasphemed. He commanded his beautiful wife Flora to do the same, but she was grieved at it, by reason of her sex and cleansed the

---

[1] "He has hindered me half a million." In fact in all respects, whether as a seller of old apparel, a doctor, nay even as a usurer, I have already shown that the Jew had to face the severest competition.

image by wiping off the filth. When the Jew noticed this he strangled his wife. The Jew was sentenced to perpetual imprisonment, but pardoned upon payment of 700 marks. This happened in the reign of Henry III. In his time a cross at Oxford was also outrageously broken and trodden upon by a mad Jew. This hatred of Christ and all that concerns him runs throughout literature. Speaking of the 'yonge folk that haunteden folye' in the Tale of the Pardoner, Chaucer says: 'Oure blissed Lordes body they totere; hem thoughte that Jewes rente hym noght ynough'. In the Ballad of the Wandering Jew (Percy's Reliques) we find: "The wicked Jewes with scoffes and scornes did dailye him (Christ) molest, that never till he left his life, our Saviour could not rest, etc. etc. I have already mentioned how in the absence of the Lord himself the Jews are said to have profaned the host of which there are several instances in the religious dramas of both England and France. No wonder that this hatred of Christ, is transferred to the Christians in literature. Thus Zariph says in *The Travels of the Three English Brothers* "The sweetest part of a Jewes feast is a Christian heart". Barabas (Act IV): "There is no music to a Christian's knell". Shylock (Act I, 3, 38): "I hate him for he is a Christian", and a great many more instances could be adduced. Some even say that *The Merchant of Venice* is only meant to show the punishment of the usurer and hater of Christians.

The Jew's Life among the Christians. — Up till now we have in the first place considered the Jew, his outward appearance, his inner being and the action emanating from him. Let us now consider how the

Christians surrounding him, act upon him; let us consider the attitude of the Christians towards the Jew. But before turning to literature let us first hear what history has to say on this point.

"The reconquest of Andalusia by the Christians associated towards the end of the 15th century with the establishment of the Inquisition, introduced a spirit of intolerance which led to the expulsion of the Jews. The consequences of this blow were momentous; it may be said to inaugurate the ghetto period"[1]. During centuries they were "outraged and oppressed, banished from this place, imprisoned in that, deprived of their money, deprived of their teeth, convicted of the most improbable crimes on the feeblest evidence, dragged at horses' tails, hanged, tortured, burned alive" and when manners became milder they were "subject to debasing restrictions and exposed to vulgar insults, locked up in particular streets in some countries, pelted and ducked by the rabble in other, excluded everywhere from magistracies and honours"[2].

In the literature the Jew is likewise shown as a constant object of oppression and persecution, which, however, is held to be a fair retribution for the atrocities perpetrated by him. Thus, for instance, after the murder of Hugh of Lincoln the avengers of the victim acted with commendable promptitude and "therefore with wilde horses he dide hem drawe and after that he heng hem by the lawe" (Chaucer, *The Prioresses Tale*)

---

[1] Enc. Britt., Vol. 15, p. 404.

[2] Macaulay, *Civil Disabilities of the Jews*. In the course of this dissertation I have already enumerated the troubles and calamities that befell the Jews during their stay in England.

On the Rialto Antonio, the gentleman-trader, calls
Shylock a misbeliever, cut-throat dog, and spits upon
his coat and beard and kicks him b e f o r e that
incident of the pound of flesh and yet asks him for the
loan of 3000 ducats and promises to do the same things
after the transaction of the business. This mode of
treatment is also found in the Jew of Malta and we
find greater and smaller injuries mentioned in other
plays. Barabas is represented as a great trader, and as
having accumulated great wealth, in this respect
literature is quite true, but it is equally true in showing
what little real pleasure the Jew derives from it.
Unwittingly it shows the hideous uncertainty of
existence lurking behind, the pitchblack background
with the shadow of death that faithful companion
of the medieval Jew, in spite of his bragging that he
is so mighty. Act III, Sc. I, 41/59, Shylock's desperate
outcry, contains in a few lines a description of the sad
fate of a Jew, a description that has not failed to
become a commonplace to every reading-man. No
Jew, as far as I know, has more eloquently and in
fewer words put down the ocean of suffering the
ancient people was weltering in, than the Christian
Shakespeare. These eighteen lines speak volumes.

The Law and the Jew. — In *Der Kampf um's Recht*
Dr. Rudolf von Ihering shows how little the Christians
cared, whether the Jew was wronged even by the judges
The Jew receives no justice [1]. In *The Merchant of*

[1] Already from their settlement in England the Jewish merchant had no
standing ground in the local courts. Throughout history they were in a fright-
fully unfavourable condition in this respect. In literature Zariph, Barabas and
Shylock all cry for law, from which I infer that they were very often fooled
and robbed of it, even before the judges.

Venice the great question is not, whether claiming a pound of flesh from a human being's body is cruel or not, at any rate this is not the great question from a *juridical* point of view. The great question is, whether Shylock has a right to it according to the laws of Venice. If the law *entitles* a man to indemnify himself in a way that is rather cruel, that man must be allowed to do the necessary things towards that indemnification. When Zariph's relations in *The Travels of the three Brothers* were sold by Christians into slavery for debt, it was a cruel thing, but the law awarded it! When Shylock wanted a pound of flesh, it was a cruel thing, but the law awarded it, and yet he was dismissed with a silly pun. The judge admits the possibility of the bond, there is nothing illegal in it! What a silly move then to deny the man to shed blood, after granting him the pound of flesh. What a silly move to allow a man to go on a certain piece of ground, but to forbid him to leave footprints on it. Besides, the Roman law, from which this custom of cutting pieces from a debtor's body is taken, did not know these scruples. In fact we get a feeling that the law of Venice is violated and that it is not the Jew Shylock who slinks away, but the typical Figure of the Jew in the Middle Ages, that pariah, the outcast of society who demanded Justice in vain. The Jews is fooled, law is given him and yet he is deceived. In confirmation of the above opinion or rather as a sort of support we read in *The Jew of Malta* (Act II) "faith is not to be held with heretics", so it is small wonder that Ithamore says (Act V) "to undo a Jew is charity, and not sin." Therefore we may without much doubt conclude what Shylock meant in Act II Sc. V. 27. "What, are there masques? Hear you me, Jessica: Lock up my door.... I swear, I have no mind of feasting forth to-night." Of Gernutus we read: "his life was like a barrow-hog, that liveth many a day: yet never once doth any good, untill men will him slay" and a little further "he cannot sleepe in rest: for feare the theife will pursue to pluck him from his nest". This thief actually appears in *The Jew of Malta*, Act III. Pilia-Borza: "Ay, but the Jew has gold, and I will have it, or it shall go hard" etc. Quite in keeping with the above, the sailors in *A Christian turned Turk*, who are not paid by their captain, steal into the house of Benwash (page 230) to recoup themselves "for to steal from a rich Jew is no more sin than to unload a weary ass." 'The Jew's eye' spoken of in *The Merchant of Venice* is thus explained. "It is worth a Jew's eye is proverbial and probably dates from the time when large ransoms were extorted by torture from the wealthy Jews in the Middle Ages by their oppressors [1]. Nor has Lorenzo any qualms of conscience in taking the wealth stolen from Shylock by Jessica. Ferneze, governor of Malta, wants money and issues the following decrees. First, the tribute money of the Turks shall all be levied amongst the Jews, and each of them to pay one half of his estate. Secondly, he that denies to pay, shall straight become a Christian. Lastly, he that denies this, shall absolutely lose all he has (Act. I). The Duke

---

[1] M. of Venice, ed. by Clark and Wright, page XXIII. It may be objected that Ithamore is not a Christian, but the Knight in the Jew of Malta holds the same opinion. Besides, Toovey declares that "it was the popular opinion that it was no sin to murder or rob an enemy of the Lord, when the murderer or robber, who was the Lord's great friend, were poor and in distress."

of Venice (Merch. IV. 1. 66) takes away all Shylock's money. "For half thy wealth, it is Antonio's; the other half comes to the general state" and yet the Duke boasts of his Christian charity in line 64. Lorenzo, Ferneze and the Duke were no thieves as Pilia-Borza or the sailors, but the end was the same for the Jew, he fell outside the scope of the law, he was outlawed.

Jew-Baiting. — Nor is the spirit of Jew-baiting absent from English literature [1], it pervades the dramas and of course we find it, where we especially expect it, in the ballad, the popular song that was sung in the streets. Having related the wickedness of Gernutus it winds up with: "Good people that doe heare this song, for truth I dare well say, that many a wretch as ill as he, doth live now at this day." Grætz, however, thinks that, seeing the factt hat there were practically no Jews in England at that time, the ballad maker meant this as a piece of moralizing, for there were in his time bloodsucking and hard-hearted usurers among the Christians and these the ballad-maker wanted to scourge, but not the Jews, nevertheless the early English ballads dealing with Christ's life and death entail Jew-baiting and in one ballad all Jews are called usurers (Rollins, p. 188).

I have looked in vain in literature for expulsion as a final despatch of the Jew, though history teems with examples. Exile may perhaps be adumbrated in the ballad of *The Wandering Jew*: "No resting could he find at all, no ease, nor hearts content; no house, nor home, nor biding place, but wandring forth he went from towne to towne in foreigne landes", or perhaps in his

---

[1] We know from history that the monks actually travelled the country to preach against the Jew.

ubiquity described in Act I of *The Jew of Malta*. In
literature, however, there is a more artistic and a
more satisfactory way of finally triumphing over the
cowardly, cunning Jew."[1] Chaucer has him drawn with
wild horses and hanged [2], Marlowe has him burned in
a cauldron, but Shakespeare beats Chancer and Marlowe.
He shows us the Jew at bay, the cunning fox with eyes
ablaze with hatred and fear. Do not forget that we live
in the time, when bear-baiting was a popular pastime,
so why should we not find Jew-baiting on the stage.
In *Gernutus* the Jew is the hog that will not do good
until men slay him. In this ballad killing a Jew is great
sport, watching his frantic movements, part of the
sport. "Gernutus now waxt franticke mad, and wotes
not what to say"! This was the very thing that was required, this was what was relished. But all this is mere
children's play, when compared with Shakespeare's
manner of dealing with the Jew. He drives him into a
corner from which there is no escape, the Jew is brought
to bay, he is baited by Gratiano, death hovers over his
head and.... does not strike. Instead of killing him,
Shakespeare kills *that* in him, without which he is
only a dirty clod thrown on a dung-hill, kills his *soul*
to the great joy and pleasure of the lookers on, and
thus we come to baptism.

Baptism. — If a man turns Christian from conviction,

[1] The New Testament tells us that the Jew was without understanding, so in
spite of all his cunning he is outdone in the end, which is contrary to history,
for in spite of everything the Jew has maintained his ground until this very
day, which, if it can not be called victory, certainly cannot be called defeat.
[2] In the Cursor Mundi þe iuu was dempt sua þat de quene / suld haue his catel
all bidene, / In hir merci his tung to take, / þat in hir curt sli missau make. /
A lion tears Gower's thieving Jew.

we may call this conversion a certain development of this man's soul. If, however, he is *compelled* in some way to become a Christian, there is no development, but a rooting up of the soul or rather a suffocation. I have already quoted authorities to prove that the Jews simply abhorred baptism and many a time and oft preferred death at the hands of their persecutors, nay even suicide to escape it. This aversion is found in literature. It is a well-known fact that the spreading of the Christian faith among the Jews has been a cherished object among the Christians [1], and it is an equally well-known fact that successes in this respect have only been sporadic. Shakespeare must be forgiven for making Shylock throw over Judaism, because the great dramatist undoubtedly knew at least one of those sporadic instances, the case of Queen Elizabeth's physician, Lopez, who had turned Christian. Such singular instances excepted, we may say: "that it was their (the Jew's) own inner life — the pure life at home, the idealism of the Synagogue, and the belief in ultimate Messianic redemption — that saved them from utter demoralization and despair." [2] Let us now turn to literature. Both Marlowe and Shakespeare (and also Daborne) put down the Jew's abhorrence of turning Christian to the lack of genuine piety and charity among the followers Jesus. This adumbrates the great

[1] In fact baptism was looked upon as the only means of reconciliation with the Jew. The Jew's aversion of baptism in spite of cruelty or kindness has always been put down to stubbornness, a quality considered to be distinctive of his race. That this stubbornness is nothing but the same loyalty of any being to any system of culture that is dear to him, could of course not be recognised in a period of fanaticism.

[2] Enc. Britt. Vol. 15, p. 405 and Friedlander, *Shakespeare and the Jew*.

struggle between Protestantism and Roman Catholicism that raged at the time and the dramatists make the Jews say things that might have been said by Protestants, but of course do not sound strange in the mouth of any non-Christian. Thus Barabas says (Act. I): "I can see no fruits in all their faith, but malice, falsehood, and excessive pride, which methinks fits not their profession". And in Act V: "This is the life we Jews are used to lead; and reason too, for Christians do the like". Rabshake in a Christian turned Turk says: "How? I turn Christian. They have Iew enough already amongst them, I turn Christian, they shall have more charity among them first" (p. 205). In *The Jew of Malta* the friars too, and in a 'Christian turned Turk' the nuns [1] are attacked covertly and openly. Thus Benwash says: "Thou thinkest our wives are such as are your holy sisters, religious Votaries", which, as appears from the context, means that his wife is chaste, but the nuns immoral and unchaste. Shakespeare makes Shylock say (Act. 11. 5. 32): "Christian fools with varnished faces" an allusion to Christian duplicity, Act I. 3. 148, "O father Abram, what these Christians are, whose own hard dealings teaches them suspect the thoughts of others!" Act. III, 1. 55. "If a Jew wrong a Christian, what is his humility? Revenge."

Yet in spite of this Shylock will be baptised, Abigail takes the veil and in the *Play of Sacrament*, a short play on the profanation of a consecrated host by the Jews, which is to be classed with the miracle-plays, the evil doers repent of their horrible deed, are converted

---

[1] 'Have not the nuns fine sport with the friars now and then' Ithamore asks? See pp. 183, 193, 200 and 202 of *The Jew of Malta* for further examples.

and baptised in the end [1]. There are those, however, who look upon this compulsory baptism from a different point of view and hold that it was the way to salvation [2]. This explanation, however, clashes with the spirit that pervades literature and moreover casts a slur on the purity of conversion. No, it must be looked upon as a punishment and not the least doubt will remain after reading that part of *The Jew of Malta*, where Fernese simply mentions baptism among other punishments. It is the final blow dealt to the hereditary enemy, the Jew.

Probability of the Character of the Jew in Literature from a Jewish Point of View. — In spite of all misrepresentation, however, there is undeniably something Jewish about the Jew in literature, there is some probability about him, although mixed with the greatest improbabilitis and absurdities. This has given rise to various opinions as to the character of the Jew in literature in its relation to reality.

Henley remarks: "Perhaps there is no character through all Shakespeare, drawn with more spirit and just discrimination, than Shylock's. His language, allusions and ideas are everywhere so appropriate to a Jew, that Shylock might be exhibited as an exemplar of that peculiar people" (quoted in the Dublin ed. of the play, 1805, p. 32).

Staunton in his Preliminary Notice to *The Merchant of Venice* speaks of "the masterly delineation of that perfect type of Judaism in olden times."

Friedlander refuting these opinions says: "This exem-

---

[1] Cambridge Hist. of English Lit., Vol. 5, p. 49.
[2] Shakespeare Jahrbuch, Vol. 53.

plar of the Jewish people I venture to call a caricature,
a travesty, a merry sport. There never was a Jew
like Shakespeare's usurer and the perfect type of
Judaism, whether in olden times or in modern times,
bears no relation whatever to Shylock. He has no likeness to the Jew of any age."

If we add to these the unprejudiced statement of
A. W. Ward [1] that the popular feeling which prevailed
in England against Jews cannot be set down as more
than continued unthinking and undiscriminating acceptance of a popular prejudice of ancient standing;
for Jews in London, during the whole of this period,
were only few in number and very little known, and
neither Shakespeare nor Marlowe is likely to have made
the acquaintance of any Jews abroad, we see that
there is no lack of diversity of opinion on this subject.
Nevertheless I cannot agree with any of these.
Staunton's view supposes all Jews in olden times to
have been so many Shylocks. Henley even goes a step
farther and thinks the modern Jews favour those of
olden times. Friedlander excludes the possibility of
a Shylock among the Jews and thus goes to the other
extreme. Ward does not consider that although there
were not many Jews in London, the dramatists may
have known the few that were there and they may
have had data that were more or less based upon observation of Jews abroad and they may have heard
some fairly good accounts of them for the English were
a well-travelled people [2]. For it cannot be denied that

[1] *Camb. Hist. of Engl. Lit.* p. 366 (Vol. 5).
[2] The dramatists themselves sometimes went abroad and may have met with
Jews. Thus we know for sure that Greene, the author of *Selimus* travelled on
the Continent, so did Nash who collaborated with Greene.

there are touches in Shylock and some other Jews that have more than a superficial character. This is also the opinion of Creizenach, Boas and Lee.

"If we detach him (Shylock) for one moment from the main incidents of the play, and picture him to ourselves, when his passions are cooled and his attention is turned to the customary pursuits of his life, we find no ordinary Italian or English merchant, but the living semblance of a Jewish trader — shrewd and covetous, it is true, but possessed of other characteristics still more distinctive of his race. Strong domestic affections, which even the cares of his counting-house cannot obscure, deep-set sympathies with the fortunes of his "tribe" and firm faith in the sacredness of its separation from the Gentiles, are traits that, combined with a pious horror of eating or drinking with Christians and a fondness of scriptural illustration, leaves little doubt in the minds of those acquainted with the peculiarities of Jewish character that they have been drawn directly from a contemporary model" [1]. Thus for instance, in Act 1. Scene III Shylock is a Jew, though perhaps not an agreeable one, in spirit and language. The bitter, morose retorts in Act IV. Scene 1 are a second instance and there are more. We find a similar state of affairs in 'A Christian turned Turk', where Rabshake with his Yiddish fun is unmistakeably Jewish (page 204). When Benwash calls out: "I am your merchant. Ruben, Rabshake, my wife, her sister fetch me 300 dukets for this Gentlemen", there is something Jewish in his loudness and fuss. There is something Jewish in his way of doing business,

[1] S. Lee, *The Original of Shylock.*

his manner of intercourse with his customers. In
Lee's opinion an attempt is made in *The Custom of
the Country* to do some justice to the Jew's racial
characteristics and this author sees an obvious reflection
of Jewish feeling in Barabas [1].

Even with this last statement I perfectly agree.
Barabas conversation with the Merchants as well as
his two monologues in the first act are Jewish in spirit
and tone. At the senate house it is exactly the same thing
and when in Act II he appears, in the night with a
light, bewailing his losses, and appeals to God to direct
the hand of Abigail, his appeal is well-worded: "O Thou,
that with a fiery pillar ledd'st the sons of Israël through
the dismal shades, light Abraham's offspring." When
he calls the Christians swine-eating creatures, heathens,
never circumcised, he avails himself of appellations not
unusual among the Jews. The author also knew something of the Jewish customs in their Synagogues, for
he speaks about the offering-basin going round there
to collect money for the poor. When Barabas buys
Ithamore in the slave-market, his way of behaving is
in conformity with the above, as is also his propensity
to cursing and his aversion to becoming a Christian.
Some have seen a Jewish trait in Shylock's sticking to
the letter of his bond. This is not quite unfounded.
The Jews are and have ever been a law-abiding people.
Their holy books were looked upon as containing the
words of God and as such were not to be trifled with, but
strictly to be obeyed, which sometimes degenerated into
a blind acceptance of the letter and it is not quite impossible that this custom did not escape the notice of

[1] See also page 75.

the Christians. I must at once add, however, that this observance of the letter was far from identical with overlooking the spirit.

From the above we may safely conclude that the dramatists based their conception of the Jew on some personal experience. In fact Boas in 'Shakespeare and his Predecessors' (p. 217) mentious a tract written between 1600 and 1625 which expressly declares 'a *store* of Jewes we have in England; *a few* in court; *many* i'the City, *more* in the country. S. Lee in 'Elizabethan England and the Jew' likewise adduces many proofs for their presence and in *The Original of Shylock*, Lee gives a full biography of Dr. Lopez, the converted Jewish physician of Queen Elizabeth, who is said to have been Shylock's prototype.

Possibility of the Jew's Character from a general Point of View. — In considering the probability of the Jew in literature, however, it is not necessary in the first place to prove, either that there have actually been Jews like Gernutus, Barabas, Shylock, etc., or that they never existed, for as I said already, art has little to do with real life. What must be considered first of all is, whether literature shows a creature and succeeds in making us look upon him as a Jew and then whether his actions are not beyond the pale of human nature in general and out of proportion to their causes in particular. If an author introduces one of his characters as a Jew and describes him as a giant-Jew or a pigmy-Jew, straight or crooked, fat or thin, fair or dark, the reader has simply to accept him, as long as the author does not tell us that this Jew has grass growing on his head or brass fingers or no entrails whatever. If our author

tells us that his Jew is an atheist, egoist, an inhuman
wretch, the worst creature on earth, we simply have to
accept him, as long as he does not tell us that his Jew
has done a thing that is utterly impossible for any living
being to do. Even when the artist shows us a Jew with
brass fingers and accordingly doing things impossible,
we have to accept him.... but.... then we may replace
the word Jew, by the word Christian, or Turk, or by
the letter x, or by any symbol, for the creature conjured
up by the artist, has lost all contact with reality in
the ordinary sense of the word and has soared into the
world of fancy, the true world of the spirit of art. It is in
this world that the Jews of literature are best lodged,
among fairies, hobgoblins, elves, dragons and whatever
the names may be of Fancy's queer offspring.

Left to the tender mercies of barbarous and semi-
barbarous peoples of Europe the Jew's fate was not
exactly a happy one. If we take for granted that he was
possessed more or less of all qualities that make up a
man, it does not strike me as improbable that one hunted
creature among the Jews, beaten out of shape mentally,
morally and physically, till he had become 'fit for treasons, stratagems and spoils', void of all that is tender and
merciful, goaded to madness by Christians, murdered a
Christian child in powerless revenge of his own massacred
dear ones. In history Shylock's words "the villany you
teach me, I will execute, and it shall go hard but I
will better the instruction", would be quite natural!
Though the 'pound of flesh' incident has been traced
to its source and has been proved of non-Jewish origin,
though it is against Jewish law and almost against
human nature, yet I should not have thought it an

utter impossibility in History, where some exasperated
and embittered Shylock may have insisted on it. If
History had recorded a Gernutus, a Shylock or even a
Barabas, I should not have been surprised at all, on the
contrary, it is more surprising that history has *not*
produced such a Jew. It almost pleads against the Jews
and reveals their true spirit out of which the theories
of the Christian faith were born [1]). As for Christian
practices or rather the practices of men who called
themselves Christians, the words of Barabas and Shylock,
that the Jew (that is the Jew of Literature) learned all
his wickedness from Christians, are perfectly true and
based on history. The Jew drains the people; very well,
but only because a Christian King drains the Jew, who
must fill his treasury. So if the Jew wants to keep something for himself, he must needs drain hard, for to use
a variant upon a certain proverb, he needs must drain
hard whom the devil drains. And yet taking everthing
into consideration he has not been so bad an extortioner, but the Christian rival could improve upon him
(Matthew Paris). If Shylock asks a pound of flesh, he
asks what a Christian had already asked before him.
A perfect howl is set up at this simple pound of flesh
demanded by a Jew, but silence reigned sublime when
the eyes, teeth and God knows what other more vital
parts of Jewish bodies were torn off by Kings and subjects, for no other consideration than that of gold, the
very same trash of which they say that the Jew is willing to sell his soul for it. No vice has been put down
to the Jew in literature, but we can demonstrate
that the Christian has been guilty of it in history,

[1] "Sufferance is the badge of our tribe" (Merchant of Venice).

before the Jew was adorned with it in literature.

Nay, I even go as far as to maintain, that, if the Jews had not had in them that peculiar characteristic of being able to suffer without striking back, just as the Jew Jesus had, but if they had had the character of a Saxon or Anglo-Norman or rather of an Italian, then tens, nay hundreds of the stamp of Barabas, the gigantic, almost grotesque villain created by Marlowe, would have arisen in history. I go a step further and say that by some freak of nature a genuine Jewish Barabas might have found a place in history, but in English literature I must object to him and his fellows. Not because I do not allow literature the same rights as history, but even because I insist upon the same rights in both, when literature pretends to be a reflection of life.

If the atrocities committed by the Jews in literature had adequate motives in literature, I should not have objected in the least, but their motives are not adequate! We all know the history of Lucifer. There is envy, followed by strife, followed by humiliation, followed by hatred, followed by revenge, followed by cruelty, a pretty logical sequence in the emotions of any creature. For every new stage there is an adequate motive. We all understand and in a way even sympathize with the devil. Was the Jew envious of anything the Christians possessed? Neither history nor literature show this. If the Jew had been envious of the Christian faith, he might have become a Christian. Of their material treasures he need not have been envious, for he was able to accumulate wealth, even better than they. So there was neither ground for spiritual nor for material envy. If the Jew hated the Christian, it was because he prevented him from earning money and did not leave him alone in religious matters, but it would not do to admit this in literature for obvious reasons. So what is this Jewish attitude based upon, what is his hate based upon in literature? What causes the Jew's daughter to murder Hugh of Lincoln? A vague feeling of hatred founded on nothing, as one only meets in hazy literature! This very same feeling, according to Marlowe's notion of art, would be a sufficient motive to make a man murder all the world. This is why we can even sympathize with the devil, but never with the Jew of literature. This is what makes the Jew in literature an absurdity.

Shakespeare, however, does not thoughtlessly consider his Jew as the traditional type of wickedness, he accounts for him psychologically, he does not, as Marlowe, try to make us believe that hatred and revenge are racial peculiarities requiring no motive. Shakespeare gives a human individual, who has been subjected to lifelong injury and yet even Shylock's revenge is not justified by what he suffers in the play. Shakespeare felt this too and therefore by way of poetical justice, the sufferings of the whole Hebrew race are more than hinted at. He makes Shylock feel the misery of a whole people, his own people, and what he suffers himself in the play, is the last drop that makes his cup of sorrow overflow, it stirs up his bile, and curdles his milk of human kindness to the sourness of hate. If we do not look at Shylock from this point of view, he becomes as ridiculous as Barabas, and it is Shakespeare's merit that he has left ample scope for this view. This,

however, Shakespeare did unintentionally, as a matter
of fact, his object was the same as Marlowe's, but being
the greater artist, his fine genius in a subtle way
frustrated his plan[1]. This is the peculiar thing about
Shakespeare's Shylock that although to all intents
and purposes he belongs to the other Jews, whose
authors committed the blunder of making them per-
petrate heinous crimes without adequate motives,
he (Shylock) was created by a mind that instinctively
shrank from such absurdity, which it felt to be against
both art and nature. This mastermind had dealt with
crimes and had always found deep psychologial problems
behind them. In this special case it would, but could
not deviate from its fine perception of art and nature
and thus it involuntarily introduced sufficient reasons
that make the Shylock-figure a possibility from a human,
but not from a Jewish point of view[2]).

Of course an artist has a right to show a man who
commits the most horrible crimes even without adequate motives, but then he enters the realms of pure
fancy, losing even the least contact with reality, and
of course these fantastic creations may be admirable.
Monsters have always been loved in art, have always
exercised a strange fascination. That some such
monster is made more hideous by the addition of the
name Jew and some exaggerated Jewish features, gives
it an additional charm. Such a monster, when created
by a great artist as Marlowe, is endowed with life as

[1] Shakesp. Jhrb., Vol. 43.
[2] In whatever way the Diaspora Jew may have retaliated upon an injury,
if he retaliated at all, it was not in this blindly passionate and unthinking
way of Shylock. His heart smarted and if he could not by force of argument
defend his right, he slunk away and patiently awaited better times.

genuine as real life, but more lasting. Shylock is among the dramatis personæ of eternity. A baby grows up and becomes an old man, whom the grave receives, but the literary monster comes fullfledged from the artist's brain and seems gifted with eternal life, and Barabas, Gernutus, Shylock, etc., wander about as so many 'wandering Jews' and woe unto the poor Jew of blood and flesh who in the least degree bears the faintest resemblance to these fatal, fantastic spirits, for thus fate has willed it, that he who resembles these monsters is the Jew par excellence: hooked nosed, long bearded, bent, grasping, fawning, etc. This is the horrible crime committed by Marlowe and his fellow artists, that they have let loose devils, who begot devils, to the everlasting torment and shame of the Jews.

If nowadays an author hatches out such a monster, it has some chance to live, but an audience of that day, accustomed as people then were to attribute all manner of atrocities to the mysterious people whom they feared as well as hated, was sure to see no improbability in Barabas or his fellows [1].

Reason of the Jew's Success on the Stage. — From the very earliest times the Jew had been in great demand on the stage. He had crucified the Lord. Love the Lord, hate the Jew. Thus it was wherever Christianity was introduced, even if the newly converted heathens had never before seen or even heard of a Jew. Not that those who preached the Gospel necessarily implied this hatred as an inevitable result, certainly not, but it is against all human nature that an ordinary creature will love the cruel murderer of his dearest friend, to

[1] *Merchant of Venice,* Clark & Wright's ed., p. XXII.

say nothing of the foul murderer of his God. This created the demand for a Jew on whom they might vent their pent up feelings and this demand was met with a supply [1].

The Jew's Change from a Comic figure to a Tragi-Comic one. — Originally the drama was a means of instructing the people. But as instruction is apt to be tedious, something comical was soon introduced to relieve the tedium. Part of this task was imposed upon the Jew. His loudness, wroth, gesticulation, face and language were eagerly made use of, he performs a grotesque dance with the accompaniment of music round the cross on which the Lord hangs. He is not a mere clown however. The peculiar thing about him is that he is not at all considered as a harmless fool and if I were to illustrate his treatment, especially in the regular drama, I could no better do so than by comparing it with a fox-hunt. The cunning fox is obnoxious, yet no sportsman will kill him, he hunts him with hounds and the fox brings all his cunning into play to throw them off his scent. But he shall not be victorious, the hounds will worry him to death under the auspices and to the satisfaction of their master. The sport is picturesque, exhilarating and accompanied by a show of danger. The whole fox-hunt has something comical about it, there is no real danger in it, it is no hunt it is a 'game', a cruel wicked game, if you just happen to be the fox, a pleasant one, if you are the hound or the hunter. So it is obvious that we must call the Jew a comic figure; at best he belongs to the region of tragi-comedy and Shakespeare one

[1] Boas, page 218.

moment makes him hover on the borderline of tragedy.
A tragi-comic figure is strictly speaking a contradiction
in terms, hence it is best fitted for the Jew whose position in the drama is also a contradiction of terms: rich
and yet poor, powerful and yet a toy in the hands of
his enemies, feared and ridiculed.

Marlowe's attempt at making him a tragic figure is
a failure. From a comic figure, as Shakespeare no doubt
wanted the Jew to be understood, Shylock has almost
changed into a tragic one; he is no longer looked upon
as a mere wretch, laughable and disgusting, but as a
human creature more sinned against than sinning, and
this our modern world has silently acknowledged. So
we see a Jew was good for many things. If he had
been a source of suffering to the Lord, his offspring,
had to atone for it by being a source of amusement
to his flock. This can be traced as far back as the Mysteries and Miracles and thence it came down to Marlowe
and Shakespeare. For in Shakespeare's native country,
during the poet's boyhood and youth, the performance
of religious plays was not yet a thing of the past.
The same holds good for Marlowe and the following
quotations [1] leave no space for doubt on this ground.
"In schools the boys performed plays. This practice
of acting plays at the Canterbury school, which has
only recently been made known,[2]) is of course specially
interesting inasmuch as Marlowe was a pupil there".
"They included scriptual subjects such as Lazarus,
Judith and Job."

[1] *Camb. Hist. of Engl. Lit.*
[1] See History of the King's School. Canterbury, by Woodruff & Cape, 1918, p. 80.

As for Shakespeare, there can be no doubt, he was familiar with Wilson's portrayal of the Jew Gerontus and Marlowe's Barabas.

Another very important factor which created a new demand for a wicked Jew in Elizabethan times, was the fact that people were induced to believe that an attempt had been made at poisoning Queen Elizabeth by her physician the Jew Lopez. Grætz and Lee have both come to the conclusion that it was the intention of Shakespeare and Marlowe to make a criminal Jew and so stigmatize all the Jews for the gratification of their patrons and the public. On the whole we may say that our early dramatists eagerly availed themselves of the popular prejudice against the conscientious adherents to the old dispensation and Shakespeare no less than the others knew what would please or diplease his audience.

Devil and Vice. — Then there was still this. The Devil and the Vice of the older drama had become stale and did no longer fit the regular drama, for which an earthly creature was wanted possessed of both. So there was a vacancy and the Jew got the post without application. The choice of the dramatists might have been worse and they made the most of their choice. Jew was already more or less synonymous with Devil, like the latter he was dark, both were accoutred in an odd way, so the step from the one to the other was after all a comparatively small one. The Jew, the villain ready made by nature, was a brilliant show and this he has remained until this very day. I have already mentioned the fusing of the Devil and the Vice with the Jew and his servant. I shall mention a few more facts that demonstrate that fusion. Nicholas Grimald represents Herod the Jewish king as having a comic fool, Gelasimus, in *Archiprophetia* 1547. In the Morality *Respublica* in 1553 Avarice is the Vice of the play. As Avarice is akin to Jew, the connection is, I think, obvious. All these things apart form no strong evidence, together ,however, they clearly show that this fusion is more than a mere supposition. In fact as late as the time of Shakespeare the clown is referred to as the Vice, and no wonder that Shakespeare sees a clown, 'the vice', in Launcelot and 'the devil' in Shylock. I am not quite sure even, whether *The Merchant of Venice* must not be looked upon as a morality or at any rate as a lineal descendant from it. Does not Antonio stand for unselfishness, love and a great many more virtues and is not Shylock the very reverse of him? Has not this play its moral just as the Morality? I think we may look upon it as a link between Shakespeare's riper work and the old drama.

An appreciation of the Jew in the Drama from a purely technical point of view. — The Jew and the Drama are inextricably connected, so much so that he may be singled out as a sample of its development. His thin and dubious shape enters the early Latin Miracles. We follow his long, gradual and unpromising formation through the Old English Miracle, where he is at best a confused unsubstantial creature, always bad. The Morality shows him again, he has lost his name, his qualities, however, stand out more clearly than ever, in fact they have come so much to the fore, that the *man* is thrown into the back ground and is almost forgotten. Then comes the drama proper and again the Jew shares

its development. Free from its chrysalis of the morality
appears a creature that is gaining in body and spirit.
We see its sudden stride forward, till it has reached
its state of full vigour and perfection in Shakespeare's
drama. But as sudden as its stride to perfection has
been, is its stride towards decay, which it practically
shares again with the temporary decay of the drama.
Obscurity, obscenity soon show us a degenerate type
lacking humanity, flesh and blood. In the Mysteries
facts from biblical history were demonstrated without
any attempt at psychological individualization and
if there was psychological individualization now and
then, it was only accidental. Every Jew is expressive of
a sort of homogenous badness and it matters little
what name he bears or whether he has any name at
all. Of course we must distinguish between the Jew
before, and the Jew contemporaneous with, or after
Jesus' stay on earth. In the morality I see a sort
of schooling of the dramatists. Like students at an
anatomical lesson, they are dissecting homogeneous
badness and laying bare its component parts, which
are chiefly the feelings and passions supposed to have
actuated the Jew against their Lord. The great
problem was now to create a being in whom those
component parts were so arranged that he was
clearly distinguishable from other beings belonging
to the same group or class and the regular drama
was the trial and partly the solution of this problem.
Leaving aside The Jew of *The Three Ladies* we shall
take Marlowe's Jew to illustrate the rise.

"Barabas, the hero, is very much more of a person
than the huge and shadowy figure of Tamburlaine,

and the action is concentrated, or at any rate confined, within a much more manageable area. But the illimitable, the apeiron of Marlowe's imagination, intimates itself, for good and for evil, here also. Although the procession of the Jew's crimes is almost as little artistic as that of Tamburlaine's triumphs and butcheries, the intensity of the poet's *personification of hatred and avarice and quasi-religious jealousy* makes it far more alive. Yet perhaps no play makes us feel so acutely and distinctly the difference between Marlowe and Shakespeare, even if we take for comparison such possibly doubtful and certainly early and immature work as Titus Andronicus. Aaron has not received the touches which make Iago and Richard, Shylock and Macbeth what they are. He has still much, and too much, about him of the mere horror-mongering which is characteristic of this middle stage of our drama, and he is, of course, much less magnificent than Barabas. But he is also much more of ahuman being" [1].

This brings us on to Shakespeare, who gives the final touch to the Jew, the Shakespearian touch, "which at once makes a character personal and individual for all time, and conveys to it the abiding characteristics of humanity which belong to no time in particular". *The Merchant of Venice* does not belong to Shakespeare's greatest and best plays but Shylock, the Jew, certainly belongs to his greatest and best creations. As for as we may speak of a perfectly developed character in literature, we must grant that Shylock is one. He stands out, fully developed, personal, individual and even with a mixed character, though not exactly a Jewish character.

[1] Saintsbury, *A Short History of English Literature*, p. 292.

Then comes the decay. Zariph is a silly attempt at repeating Shylock and an utter failure. As for *A Christian turned Turk*, the play itself is a huge piece of sensationalism, loose morality, foulness of language, forced situations, and the Jew is made to fit them all.

The last statement may be generalised and we may safely say all the Jews in the dramas of the decay period are made to fit the plays and show a degeneration of a degeneration

THE END.

CONCLUSION

I have traced the Jew, as he figures in Early English Literature, his bearing and facial expression, his dress, his house, his money, his soul, his intellect, his religion, his family, his friends, his servants, his philanthropy, his attitude towards the Christians, his life among them, his trade, etc., even his very nose. As far as possible in this short essay, I have also traced him in most of these respects, as he figures in History. On the whole I have come to the conclusion that he has been misrepresented partly on purpose on account of intolerance and fanaticism on the side of the authors, partly in a bona-fide manner, because the artists knew no better. He resembles the Jew in history as much as the chimeras of the Notre Dame resemble a human creature, which in some grotesque way they do. As regards the Jew's prosecution, however, literature is a pretty correct, though somewhat weak reflection of history. En passant it tells us that he was scorned, his laws taunted, his trade hampered, his wife or daughter violated, his Synagogue prophaned, that he was even sold into slavery (See *The Travels of the Three Brothers*), which is not yet a complete catalogue of his sufferings. As for the artistic value of the various Jews in literature, I deem it sufficient to say that their artisticity is related to, and in strict concord with the genius of their creators, the unknown ballad-maker,

Daborn, Marlowe, Shakespeare, etc. The fact that the great Dutch actor Bouwmeester is still applauded as Shylock, is better able to demonstrate Shylock's artistic value than any words of mine.

We know little if anything about ourselves, we know less about others and least about the theatre figure, but we imagine we know much about ourselves, more about others and all about the theatre figure. The best painter, the best sculptor is able to give us, only a vague image of what we might call man proper and the best author can give no more. These shadowy reflections, hollow and sketchy as they are, have, however, obtained a relatively great value in real life and therefore it is important that there should be no foul play in their creation, and foul play there was. For due note must be paid to the fact that only non-Jews have created our Jew, Christian authors were at work instigated by racial hatred, fanaticism and prejudices, which in itself would already condemn the shadowy reflection of the Jew as absolutely untrue. For just as we can only make up the being of any nation by its own collective literature as the utterance of its soul, thus we could only make up the being of the Jews by their own collective literature as the utterance of their soul. The soul of a nation must needs be contorted, when seen through the medium of an author belonging to an other nation and an other race, however honest he may be in his attempt in showing it. The English artists were not even honest in their attempt and this is why their Jews are perfectly distorted creatures. When the Jews were still one nation, they created a literature of their own. In this literature we find bad

Jews and good Jews. By the side of the bad ones we find the heroic figures of Moses, David, Solomon, Job, the prophets and many more, nor is there a lack of heroines. Many of these heroes and heroines have inspired Christian artists. Let us hope for the Jews that there will again come a time, when they will have a country of their own, a civilization of their own, a literature of their own and then Shylock will change like the Beast of the Fairy Tale into some beautiful prince, when the charm cast over him by the Witch of Malevolent Ignorance and Injustice, will be dispelled by Beauty, the Beauty of Love, Understanding and Justice.

PRINCIPAL BOOKS, PAMPHLETS, PERIODICALS, TEXTS, ESSAYS,
LITERARY HISTORIES, BOOKS OF REFERENCE, REFERRED TO

F. S. Boas, Shakespeare and his Predecessors, London, 1902.
Beaumont and *Fletcher*. The Custome of the Country, London, 1904.
Ben Jonson, The Fox, London, 1915.
W. Carew Hazlitt, Old English Plays, London, 1874.
Catalogue of the Anglo-Jewish Historical Exhibition by Jacobs and Wolf
      London, 1888.
Chaucer, Prioresses Tale. Oxford, 1915.
G. L. A. Craik, A Manual of Engl. Literature and Language, Leipzig, 1874.
W. Creizenach, Betrachtungen über den Kaufman von Venedig.
     „   Geschichte des neueren Dramas. IV. Halle a. S., 1916.
Cambridge History of English Literature.
F. J. Child, English and Scottish Popular Ballads, London, 1904.
G. G. Coulton, Social Life in Britain from the Conquest to the Reformation.
      Cambridge, 1918.
Robert Daborne, A Christian turned Turke, ed. by Prof. Dr. A. E. H. Swaen.
      Anglia XX.
Day, Rowley and *Wilkins*. The Travailes of the Three English Brothers.
Dictionary of National Biography.
Earle and *Plummer*, Two Saxon Chronicles Parallel, Oxford, 1892, 1899.
Encyclopaedia Britannica.
The Jewish Encyclopaedia.
G. Friedlander, Shakespeare and the Jew, London, 1921.
Hugo Gilbert, Robert Green's Selimus, Diss. Kiel, 1899.
J. R. Green, A Short History of the English People, London, 1919.
H, Graetz, Shylock in den Sagen, in den Dramen und in der Geschichte, Kroto-
      schin 1899.
     „   Geschichte der Juden, Leipzig 3e Auflage, 1890/4.
Wm. Heming, The Jewes Tragedy, herausgegeben von H. A. Cohn, Bang's Ma-
      terialen XL, 1913.
Dr. Rudolf von Ihering. Der Kampf um's Recht, Wien, 1884.
Jewish Quarterly Review.
Jahrbuch der Deutschen Shakespeare Gesellschaft.
L. Kellner, Die Quellen von Marlowe's Jew of Malta (Engl. Studiën, X) 1886.
E. Koeppel, Konfessionelle Strömungen (Shakespeare Jahrb. XL s. XVI—
      XXIX).
S. Lee, The Original of Shylock (Gentleman's Magazine 1880).

S. Lee, Elizabethan England and the Jews (New Shakespeare Soc. Transactions 1887/92).

Ch. Lamb, The Essays of Elia, London, 1910.

Marlowe, The Jew of Malta, London, 1914.

Mary Magdalene, The Life and Repentance of, The Tudor Facsimile Texts, London, 1908.

Massinger, The Duke of Milan (The Works of the British Dramatists, ed. by J. S. Keltic, Edinburgh 1873.

J. Meissner, Die englische Komödianten zur Zeit Shakespeare in Oesterreich. Beiträge zur Geschichte d. deutschen Literatur Bd. IV. 1884.

Wilhelm Meyer, Der Wandel des Jüdischen Typus in der englischen Literatur, Diss., Marburg a. L. 1912.

H. H. Milman, The History of the Jews, London, 1863.

Macaulay, History of England, Leipzig, 1849.

„   Crit. and Hist. Essays, On Machiavelli and Civil Disabilities of the Jews, Leipzig, 1850.

I. Münz, Uber die Jüdischen Ärzte im Mittelalter. Frankfurt a. M., 1922.

The Oxford Dictionary.

George Peele, David and Bethsabe. The Works of the British Dramatists, ed. by J. S. Keltie, Edinburgh 1873.

A. W. Pollard, English Miracle Plays. Oxford, 1909.

Th. Percy, Reliques of Ancient English Poetry, Leipzig, 1866.

Roxburghe Ballads, printed for the Ballad Society, London, 1871—1897.

Shakespeare, The Merchant of Venice, Oxford, 1895.

D. Strumpf, Die Juden in der mittelalterlichen Mysterien-, Mirakel- und Moralitäten-Dichtung Frankreichs. Diss. Ladenburg a. N., 1920.

D' Blossiers Tovey, Anglia Judaica, Oxford, 1738.

Transactions of the New Shakespeare Soc. 1875/6.

A. W. Ward, History of English Dramatic Literature to the Death of Queen Anne, London, 1875.

R. Wasserman, Beruf, Konfession und Verbrecher. Eine Studie über die Kriminalität der Juden in Vergangenheit und Gegenwart, München 1907.

I. Zollschan, Das Rassenproblem unter besonderer Berücksichtigung der theoretischen Grundlage der jüdische Rassenfrage. Wien u. Leipzig 1910, 1912.